the PlantPure kitchen

the PlantPure kitchen

130 Mouthwatering Whole Food Recipes and Tips for a Plant-Based Life

KIM CAMPBELL

with Whitney Campbell

Photos by Colin Campbell

BenBella Books, Inc.
Dallas, TX

BenBella

10440 N. Central Expressway, Suite 800 | Dallas, TX 75231
www.benbellabooks.com | Send feedback to feedback@benbellabooks.com

Printed in the United States of America
10 9 8 7 6 5 4 3 2 1

Library of Congress Cataloging-in-Publication Data

Names: Campbell, Kim (Nutritionist), author. | Campbell, Whitney, 1991-
   author. | Campbell, Colin, 1993- photographer.
Title: The Plantpure Kitchen : 130 mouthwatering Whole Food recipes and tips
   for a plant-based life / Kim Campbell with Whitney Campbell ; photos by
   Colin Campbell.
Description: Dallas, TX : BenBella Books, Inc., [2017] | Includes
   bibliographical references and index.
Identifiers: LCCN 2016037698 (print) | LCCN 2016049924 (ebook) | ISBN
   9781944648343 (trade paper : alk. paper) | ISBN 9781944648213 (electronic)
Subjects: LCSH: Cooking (Natural foods) | Vegan cooking. | Nutrition. |
   LCGFT: Cookbooks.
Classification: LCC TX741 .C354 2017 (print) | LCC TX741 (ebook) | DDC
   641.5/636—dc23
LC record available at https://lccn.loc.gov/2016037698

Editing by Leah Wilson and
   Madison Heim-Jinivisian
Copyediting by Karen Wise
Proofreading by Cape Cod Compositors, Inc. and
   Jenny Bridges
Indexing by WordCo Indexing Services, Inc.
Text design by Aaron Edmiston
Text composition by Silver Feather Design
Front cover by Kit Sweeney
Full cover by Sarah Dombrowsky
Printed by Versa Press

Photos by Colin Campbell unless otherwise
   noted.
Photo on page 145 ©iStockPhoto/Denio Rigacci
Photo on page 16 ©iStockPhoto/
   Janine Lamontagne
Photo on page 17 ©iStockPhoto/
   Barbara Helgason
Photo on page 100 ©iStockPhoto/
   Steve Debenport
Photos on pages 1, 11, 23, 43, 45, 61, 81, 99, 125,
   165, 219, and 239 from Pexels.com

Distributed by Perseus Distribution | www.perseusdistribution.com
To place orders through Perseus Distribution:
Tel: (800) 343-4499 | Fax: (800) 351-5073 | E-mail: orderentry@perseusbooks.com

Special discounts for bulk sales (minimum of 25 copies) are available.
Please contact Aida Herrera at aida@benbellabooks.com.

Contents

Page 26

Page 41

Page 68

Page 91

Appetizers, Dips, and Spreads

Page 114

Soups and Stews

Page 104

Entrées

Page 140

Page 132

Page 147

Page 197

Page 205

Page 186

Sides

Desserts 239

Page 230

Page 248

Page 252

Page 259

Foreword

That I have been asked to write this foreword suggests I am somewhat of an expert in the contents of this book—even though, normally, I hardly know what is in a kitchen, let alone how to make a meal in one! But I will claim expertise because I have many times eaten the food that this book's author, my daughter-in-law Kim Campbell, prepares, made according to the recipes in this book. Kim is simply a very good cook. She is a natural who goes into the kitchen, looks to see what food she has in the fridge, and then just imagines what could go together to make a good meal. Her food is just plain good—with the added value of being exceptionally healthy.

Kim's food was used in the immersion meal programs in the 2015 documentary film, *PlantPure Nation* (now on Netflix), which shows the positive impact on health people get when eating food from this book. For those who have come to this book without having seen the film, I invite you to watch the film, too, so that you may see just a few of these amazing health benefits.

I am a scientist doing experimental research on food and health, and have gradually come to know, over these past six decades of my research career, the whole food, plant-based diet's awesome capacity to make people well—a capacity far beyond what I ever thought possible. I am talking not only about preventing disease but treating or actually reversing disease.

I know that, for many people, transitioning to this dietary lifestyle may be difficult—for a variety of reasons. It's not easy to change lifelong eating habits when we have taste preferences to which we have long been accustomed. But know that our customary preferences for food can actually change within a period even as short as a month or two, during which time the health benefits become obvious.

For anyone truly interested not just in preventing future health problems but also in reversing present health problems, I suggest that you treat yourself to this book. Stick with these recipes for at least a couple months and you will see for yourself the benefits. I believe you'll be pleasantly surprised.

—T. Colin Campbell
September 2016

Introduction

In 2015, *The PlantPure Nation Cookbook* was published, and the film *PlantPure Nation* was released in theaters in over 100 cities and towns across North America. Since then, life has been a whirlwind. As part of the team behind the film and the grassroots community spreading the message of plant-based nutrition, my husband, Nelson Campbell, and I have had the opportunity to travel to many cities, meet wonderful people, hear inspiring stories, and grow our PlantPure family. Here are just a few of the other happenings at PlantPure in the year since the film's release: the creation of hundreds of active "PlantPure Pods" across North America and overseas that are helping to spread the message of plant-based nutrition and build community; ground-breaking partnerships with large health-care systems in Florida and Texas; development of a 21-day Jumpstart program that enables people to learn about and experience the benefits of a plant-based diet; and the creation of a line of plant-based frozen entrées, a second *Kitchen Starter* line of products for the preparation of fresh meals, a stream of inspiring and educational videos, a magazine, a smartphone app, a new film project, and more. It's been a fun and rewarding adventure, and I truly love the role I have been given within our organization: culinary education and recipe development.

As I do this work, teaching people about the benefits of plant-based eating and helping them change their diets, I always try to remember how my own family got to this point. We have practiced a whole food, plant-based lifestyle for nearly 30 years, but it was never without struggles and mistakes. Nelson and I raised three kids and led busy lives, and we fell short in the diet department more times than I care to admit. But whenever we made unhealthy decisions, they were because of habit or the kind of neglect that comes from feeling stressed and rushed. I believe that no one is perfect; to err is human!

My kids often remind me, "Mom, remember when you made that cake with gelatin and oil?" Or, "Mom, remember the candy in our Easter baskets and Christmas stockings?" I cringe a little, but I share the same memories.

It is these memories that remind me of the importance of humility. I feel strongly that a judgmental, extremist attitude can be an impediment to building a plant-based world. Every day that this lifestyle becomes more accepted by physicians, researchers, and regular people everywhere, it becomes easier for everyone. But we need to remember that as others begin this journey, many will make mistakes. And if you are one of those people just starting, it's okay if you don't always do as well as you would like. Just try your best, and as you gain knowledge and experience, over time you will get where you want to go. I remember exactly how we too just jumped in, fingers first at times, without knowing exactly what we were doing. As a community we need to encourage, not judge.

It has helped in my own journey that cooking is my passion. And I am always researching the latest information about processed foods, labeling, whole foods, organic versus conventional, GMOs, sugar, oil, salt, and other issues of our day. The food and agricultural industries have often left the consumer with a convoluted mess to figure out. If I had one easy recommendation to make from all these experiences, it is this: The more you stick with whole foods while minimizing highly processed foods, and shop for and prepare you own food rather than dining out, the more health benefits you will enjoy.

This cookbook is a compilation of more recipes that are typical in our home and also part of our ongoing Jumpstarts. It especially focuses on "main meals" since I had many requests for some of the recipes that we provide either in our frozen line or PlantPure Kitchen Starters. I am always excited to share any recipe that will promote good health. In addition, the majority of these recipes are gluten free or easy to adapt. It is my personal mission to continue providing recipes that make this lifestyle easy, delicious, and sustainable, and my goal with this cookbook is to provide people with the knowledge, tools, and recipes to build delicious plant-based meals that are both healthy and fun.

Food is truly how we celebrate and enjoy life. At every holiday, birthday, ball game, church event, and other celebration, we want to serve delicious food that people can enjoy. Why? Because food makes us excited, happy, and, most of all, comforted. I love my work creating and sharing healthy, great-tasting food for just that reason. I hope you can find a few new favorite recipes in this book, adapt them to your preferences, share them, and prepare them regularly for the ones you love. Eat well and love life!

—Kim Campbell

Getting
Started

Plant-Based Pantry Items for the Beginner

When our kids moved into their first apartments, I took on the task of building their kitchen pantries. It wasn't easy because they were starting from ground zero.

The following list is where we started to help them begin their cooking journeys. If you're just starting on your own plant-based cooking journey, you can use this list to make sure you have the basics. (For a more comprehensive and educational look at a larger variety of pantry options, see "Building Your PlantPure Pantry" in *The PlantPure Nation Cookbook*.)

Legumes

Black beans, black-eyed peas, cannellini beans, chickpeas (garbanzo beans), Great Northern beans (navy beans), lentils, pinto beans, red kidney beans, split peas

Dried Herbs and Spices

Basil, black pepper, cayenne pepper, chipotle chile powder, chives, cinnamon (ground and whole sticks), cloves (ground and whole), cumin (ground and whole seeds), curry powder, dill, fennel seeds, garam masala, garlic powder, ginger (ground), Italian herb blend, mustard (ground and whole seeds), nutmeg (ground and whole), Old Bay Seasoning, oregano, paprika (smoked and regular), parsley, rosemary, sage, sea salt, thyme, turmeric (ground)

Frozen Produce

Bell peppers, berries, broccoli, cauliflower, corn, edamame, greens (spinach, kale, Swiss chard, collard greens, etc.), mango, mixed fruit, onions, peas

Note: Frozen produce is flash frozen after harvesting, which means that the nutrients are preserved. Frozen is the next best option to fresh.

Grains, Flours, and Grain Products

Brown rice, bulgur wheat, oats, quinoa, whole wheat couscous, whole wheat flour, whole wheat pastry flour

Nuts, Nut Butters, and Seeds

Almonds and almond butter, cashews, chia seeds, flaxseeds and flax meal, peanuts and peanut butter, poppy seeds, pumpkin seeds, sesame seeds, sunflower seeds, tahini, walnuts

Sweeteners

Agave nectar, pure maple syrup, Medjool dates, molasses, Sucanat

Tofu and Tempeh

Note: It's important to always buy organic tofu and tempeh since many soy products are often GMO foods.

Vinegars, Condiments, and Sauces

Apple cider vinegar, balsamic vinegar, red wine vinegar, rice vinegar, white vinegar

Dijon mustard, ketchup (low sodium/ sugar), lemon juice, lime juice, miso paste, sriracha, yellow mustard

Tamari (low sodium), Worcestershire sauce (vegan)

Whole-Grain Pasta

Brown rice pasta, corn pasta, farro pasta, kamut pasta, quinoa pasta, soba noodles, whole-grain pasta with sprouted wheatgrass, whole wheat pasta

Note: Make sure the pasta you buy is made from 100 percent whole grains, rather than traditional white pasta, which lacks fiber and many nutrients. Some whole-grain pasta, like brown rice pasta, is gluten-free, an added benefit for those who do not eat gluten.

Miscellaneous

Coconut milk (canned lite), cornstarch, nori sheets, nutritional yeast flakes, tomatoes (canned, diced and whole), tomato paste (canned), vegetable broth (canned or boxed, low sodium)

Your Guide to Unfamiliar Plant-Based Ingredients

Jackfruit

Jackfruit is a starchy, fibrous fruit popular among plant-based eaters because the texture of green (unripened) jackfruit makes it a fantastic meat substitute. Jackfruit is native to Southeast Asia—where one tree can produce up to 200 fruits a year—so it is not surprising that green jackfruit is used in a variety of curry dishes.

You can find this unusual fruit at Asian food stores and even in the vegan section of some big supermarkets. I recommend you buy it in a can packed in water. It is usually reasonably priced at about $2 a can. If you have your heart set on buying it fresh, be aware that finding it green may be difficult, and ripe jackfruit cannot be substituted for green. In addition, working with fresh jackfruit can be quite messy and sticky, so you may want to research this process a bit before diving in.

Miso

Miso is a Japanese fermented soybean paste with a salty, tangy flavor that adds depth and savoriness to sauces, soups, and dressings. Miso ranges in color from light brown to dark red varieties; the darker the color, the stronger the flavor.

To create miso, soybeans are combined with salt and a mold known as koji, then aged for up to 24 months to create a rich, savory paste. Miso can also be made from barley, rice, chickpeas, and other legumes; each one tastes slightly different.

You can find miso in the produce department of many grocery stores in a plastic tub. It will keep in your refrigerator for up to a year.

Nutritional Yeast

Nutritional yeast, commonly known as "nooch," can be found in the bulk section of natural food stores. These dark yellow flakes add a nutty, cheesy flavor to recipes and can also be sprinkled on popcorn, salads, sauces, soups, gravies, pastas, casseroles, and sandwiches. Nutritional yeast is a low-fat, low-sodium, non-GMO food that contains no salt, wheat, corn, soy, milk, or egg.

Nutritional yeast is a member of the fungi family, just like mushrooms. It is made from a single-celled organism that is grown on cane and beet molasses for about seven days. During the growing period, B vitamins are added to provide the yeast with the nutrients it needs to grow. The yeast is then harvested, pasteurized, and heat dried, which deactivates the organism.

Tamari

Tamari, the Japanese version of soy sauce, is a byproduct of fermented soybeans. Both tamari and soy sauce add salt to a recipe. The main difference between the two is the use of wheat—tamari is wheat-free and gluten-free.

Tamari and soy sauce are interchangeable in recipes, but I prefer the flavor of tamari. Tamari is thicker, slightly darker, smoother, and less salty than soy sauce. I like to think of tamari as the "gentler," mellower version of soy sauce. Whichever one you choose, look for a low-sodium variety.

Seitan

Seitan is made almost entirely from wheat gluten—the protein portion of wheat flour. It is sometimes referred to as "wheat meat" because of its meaty, chewy texture. Seitan is typically flavored in various ways to mimic sausage, chicken, or beef.

I do not recommend seitan since it is a highly processed food that often causes digestive issues in many individuals.

Tempeh and Tofu

Both tempeh and tofu are made from soybeans. However, they are quite different in flavor, texture, and appearance.

Tofu: Tofu is made by coagulating soy milk. A salty or acidic solution is added to the milk to create curds, which are then pressed and separated from the remaining liquid to create tofu. Tofu does not have a strong flavor alone but absorbs the flavors you add to it extremely well. It comes in many textures—silken, soft, firm, and extra-firm—and can be baked, sautéed, and blended. Silken works best for making creamy sauces and smoothies. For other uses, I prefer extra-firm because you get more tofu for your money. Softer tofu has more water content, so you are essentially buying water.

Tempeh: Tempeh is made by mixing soybeans, sometimes combined with rice, with the spores of a fungus, putting them in a moist warm environment, and allowing the fungus to grow. The fermentation process creates a thick white cake around the beans. Tempeh has a very firm texture and a mild nutty flavor. Similar to tofu, it takes on the flavor of the sauce you put it in. I recommend slicing and marinating tempeh overnight in the sauce of your choice. You can usually find tempeh in the produce section of the grocery store next to the tofu. There are many tempeh brands and flavors, so try a few to see what you like best.

Kitchen Tools and Gadgets

Cooking has always been my biggest pleasure, but not having the right kitchen tools can make it stressful. It's not always easy to figure out which tools are the right ones—there are so many to choose from. It can be tempting to buy something that you don't actually need, which can be a problem if what you are buying is expensive or if your kitchen is tight on storage space.

That pasta maker we bought 25 years ago was a major purchase made with good intentions, but I think I've used it a dozen times at most. Then there was the food dehydrator, stand mixer, waffle iron, sandwich maker, apple slicer/corer, spiralizer, electric knives, sprouting trays, beer maker, popcorn machine, juicer, soy milk maker, rice cookers, Yonana machine, flour mill, and a few more that slip my mind. Some of these gadgets have been used once or twice over the years, while others have found their way to the attic or local thrift store.

Here's the good news, since kitchen tools aren't cheap: You don't need much to be a fantastic plant-based cook—just a few essentials. Here's a list of my most frequently used items:

Knives: Invest in at least three good knives: a small paring knife, a larger utility knife (not too large, though—make sure it fits comfortably in your hand), and a serrated bread knife. Using high-quality, sharp knives saves time, not to mention fingers. I also recommend buying a sharpening stone and learning how to use it properly. There are plenty of YouTube videos that can teach you how.

Cutting Boards: Cutting boards help preserve your knives and countertops. My favorite boards are bamboo because they are easy on my knives and lightweight, thus easy to store—although I keep one on my kitchen island since we are almost always cutting something.

Peelers: I use traditional peelers more than once a day and replace them periodically, as they dull over time. We peel carrots, cucumbers, potatoes, and squash often. A julienne peeler has small teeth built into the blade; it is used to create matchstick-style carrots or zucchini shreds. I recommend having both of these peeler styles.

Whisks: I recommend having two or three different sizes of whisk. I use a very small one for small mixtures and larger ones for soups and sauces. I prefer silicone whisks because they do not scratch bowls or pans, but some people prefer metal; metal whisks are a bit stiffer than silicone, so they produce a better whip.

Silicone Nonstick Baking Mats: These durable mats allow for oil-free baking without the use of parchment paper or aluminum foil. They come in a variety of sizes and can withstand temperatures up to about 500°F. They also reduce cleanup time, and can be rolled up for easy storage.

Measuring Spoons and Cups: You can never have too many measuring spoons.

I love having more than one set because I use them a lot, so they are often wet or dirty. I prefer stainless steel for measuring spoons because it does not rust, crack, or discolor. You will also need a set (or two!) of dry measuring cups (again, I prefer stainless steel), as well as a glass or clear plastic measuring cup for liquids.

Food Processor: This is my most used kitchen tool. I use it for chopping nuts, mincing veggies, making bread crumbs, and preparing everything from smooth sauces to chunky salsas. I started out with a food processor my mom purchased at a church bazaar and loved it so much that after a few years use I went out and bought a nice Cuisinart, which has never let me down.

High-Powered Blender: I recommend a Vitamix—an investment for sure, but they last forever and are well worth the cost. I bought a refurbished machine over seven years ago and it still runs like a dream. If that is not in your budget, a similar but less expensive option is the NutriBullet, which we purchased for our kids for their college years. It's smaller and less powerful than the Vitamix, but it still does the job. Either will let you easily make mayonnaise, smoothies, and creamy dressings, and sauces.

Pots, Pans, and Baking Dishes: You will want to have a few stainless steel pots and pans in various sizes: a couple of small and medium saucepans with lids, a couple of larger stockpots with lids, and at least one good nonstick skillet. You'll also need a few metal, glass, or ceramic baking dishes of different sizes, and a couple of aluminum rimmed baking sheets.

Nonessential but Fun and Helpful Gadgets

Pressure Cookers and Slow Cookers: These appliances both save you time and really help build flavors in dishes. A pressure cooker speeds up the cooking process; see page 146 for more information on my favorite pressure cooker, the Instant Pot. A slow cooker, on the other hand, allows for hands-off cooking while you are sleeping or at work.

Microplane: A Microplane rasp grater is a great tool for grating ginger, garlic, and citrus zest. It also lets you turn a block of chocolate into pretty little sprinkles for garnishing pies and ice creams. You can even use a Microplane to grate chiles for smaller bits of heat.

Nut Milk Bag: There is nothing healthier than fresh almond milk! (See my recipe on page 34.) If you make your own almond or other nut milks, I highly recommend a nut milk bag for straining out the nut pulp to make a smoother milk. They are easy to clean and reusable. Your local natural food market may carry nut milk bags, but I've found that Amazon offers the widest variety.

Produce Chopper: I have the Vidalia Chop Wizard, which chops or dices fruits and vegetables in two different sizes. It's fast, safe, and easy, making meal prep a cinch.

French Fry Cutter: We love French fries made from both regular white potatoes and sweet potatoes, and a French fry cutter makes the prep quick and easy. I recommend the three-in-one tool from Savant Kitchen that has one blade for cutting French fries, one for coring and slicing apples, and one for pitting and halving mangoes.

If you have an urge to buy something not on these lists but are not sure you will use it, I recommend looking for used items online or taking a trip to your local thrift store. I have often found food processors, waffle irons, and ice cream makers there. Picking up an item cheap is a great way to discover if you truly need it; if you find you use it often, you can always purchase the new, higher-end version later.

Everyday Plant-Based Substitutions

If you want to prepare a traditional recipe that includes non-plant-based ingredients, here are some easy substitutions.

Egg

Substitutions for One Egg
1 tablespoon flax meal + 3 tablespoons water (allow to thicken for 10 minutes)
1 tablespoon chia seeds + 3 tablespoons water (allow to thicken for 10 minutes)
2 tablespoons cornstarch + 3 tablespoons water
2 tablespoons arrowroot + 3 tablespoons water
¼ cup unsweetened plant-based yogurt
3 tablespoons aquafaba (the juice left over from cooked or canned beans)
¼ cup silken tofu (best for baking)
⅓ cup unsweetened applesauce (best for baking)
¼ cup pureed banana, prune, or baby food fruits (pears, apricots, blueberries) (best for baking)

Oils and Butter

For Sautéing: When sautéing veggies that have a good amount of water in them, such as onions, you can simply dry sauté, adding very small amounts of water as they cook if needed to deglaze the pan. Both onions and bell peppers caramelize beautifully without added fat.

For other vegetables, try one of the following instead of oil or butter:

Low-sodium vegetable broth
Water
Wine
Juice

For Baking: In baking, oil and butter are used to emulsify and soften the final product. Here are some great 1:1 substitutions that can play the same role:

Applesauce (unsweetened)
Mashed bananas
Pureed prunes or baby food fruits (pears, apricots, blueberries)
Soft or silken tofu

For Making Dressings and Sauces: Nuts, nut butters, avocados, and seeds are great substitutions for fat in dressings and sauces because they have just enough natural oils in them to emulsify and thicken a dressing. You don't need much to make a difference, and you are still getting the whole food with all its nutrients and fiber mixed in! Try these:

Substitutions for ¼ Cup Oil
¼ cup raw nuts + ¼ cup water
¼ cup nut butter + ¼ cup water
½ cup mashed avocado + ¼ cup water

Dairy Milk

I recommend trying a variety of plant-based milks and sticking with the ones that you like and that are easy to access and affordable. You can even make your own—see my recipe for almond or cashew milk on page 34. Here's a partial list of plant-based milk options; be sure to always buy them unsweetened:

Almond
Cashew
Flax
Hazelnut
Hemp
Oat
Rice
7-Grain
Soy

Cheese

Cheese is loaded with saturated fats and casein, the milk protein that is linked to cancer and other diseases. The flavor and texture of many cheeses are often hard to replicate, so most of the time I just leave cheese out of a recipe and add more veggies. When I do want a cheese sauce or filler, I use these substitutions:

Cheese sauces: This cookbook has recipes for a Spicy Nacho Sauce (page 140) and a Welsh Rarebit sauce (page 216) that are great stand-ins for dairy cheese sauce.

Make some ahead of time, store it in the fridge, and use it on top of your favorite dishes. *The PlantPure Nation Cookbook* offers a recipe for cauliflower Alfredo sauce that makes a wonderful topper as well.

Grated Parmesan: Grind up walnuts or any other nut you choose, then add bread crumbs and nutritional yeast in equal amounts.

Ricotta: *The PlantPure Nation Cookbook* has a delicious tofu ricotta recipe that tastes and looks similar to real ricotta and can be used in a variety of recipes.

I recommend avoiding the commercial vegan cheese products on the market since most of them are very high in processed oils.

Meat

If you are looking for something to add a bit more substance to a casserole, stew, or stir-fry, here are some suggestions:

Green jackfruit: When cooked, green jackfruit (see page 4) has a similar texture to pulled pork. Be sure to buy only canned green (unripened) jackfruit, packed in water.

Lentils and beans: Lentils and beans come both dried and canned and in many sizes. You can add them to a dish whole or slightly mashed to add a thicker, heartier consistency. Lentils and beans are the ideal choice for burritos, chilis, and hearty soups or stews.

Mushrooms: There are many varieties of mushrooms available even at regular supermarkets these days, and they all absorb flavor well and add a pleasant chewiness. I usually choose shiitake mushrooms when I am going for a meaty texture. Large portobello mushroom caps make hearty grilled "burgers."

Soy Curls: Butler Soy Curls are 100 percent soybeans, with no added ingredients. They come dried and require soaking in water before use; they become chewy when rehydrated. The only place I know to purchase them currently is through Amazon.

Tofu and tempeh: Both tofu and tempeh can add meatiness to your dishes, but you will need to bake them to achieve a chewy texture. Marinate tofu or tempeh in your favorite sauce and then bake in a 400°F oven until golden brown and dry to the touch.

Bulgur wheat: Bulgur wheat adds a nice bulky texture to stews and chilis. It absorbs flavors well, so you don't need much seasoning. I recommend adding ¼ to ½ cup of uncooked bulgur to a stew or chili that serves four.

Gluten-Free Alternatives

If you're avoiding gluten—whether because you're gluten sensitive or gluten intolerant—the good news is that simply avoiding processed foods will eliminate most of the gluten from your diet. If you're gluten sensitive, you may also want to read the section on ancient grains on page 44.

If you need a gluten-free substitute for recipes in this book or beyond, use this guide:

Ingredient Containing Gluten	Gluten-Free Alternative
Soy sauce	Tamari
Whole wheat tortilla wraps or bread	Gluten-free wraps and breads (just be sure to check the label for eggs and oil content!)
Hoisin sauce	Homemade Hoisin Sauce (see recipe on page 97)
Whole wheat flour or pastry flour	Gluten-free oat flour*
Whole wheat bread crumbs	Crumbled gluten-free pretzels, crackers, bread, or corn tortillas
Panko bread crumbs	Ground-up Corn Flakes cereal or crumbled Rice or Corn Chex
Bulgur wheat	Buckwheat groats, brown rice couscous, or quinoa
Whole wheat orzo	Short-grain brown rice or quinoa
Whole wheat pasta	Corn, quinoa, or brown rice pastas

*Note that while gluten-free oat flour will work for almost any recipe calling for wheat flour, yeast breads are the exception. Yeast breads are very difficult to make gluten-free. It can be done—there are many gluten-free yeast bread recipes out there—but they generally require extra ingredients to achieve the proper texture.

Additionally, be aware that while oats are naturally gluten-free, many are processed in plants contaminated with gluten from wheat and other grains. If you have a severe gluten sensitivity or suffer from gluten intolerance, you should look for oats processed in a gluten-free facility. Bob's Red Mill has a certified 100 percent gluten-free oat flour.

Meal Planning and Organization

I find the key to successful meal planning is being organized in the kitchen. Working at PlantPure, teaching our kids how to cook, writing cookbooks, and teaching cooking classes have forced me to organize myself in ways I never thought possible. Here are a few personal strategies and habits that make my job and life easier (and can save money, too!):

- **Clean out your refrigerator weekly.** This gives you the opportunity to use up or discard older food and organize your space to make room for new produce. There's nothing worse than arriving home with bags of groceries and no place to store them. And if your refrigerator is packed full, most likely there is something rotting somewhere in the chaos.

- **Make a meal plan for the week.** Plan meals that allow you to eat all the produce and other food in your refrigerator. Include the kids in this step and even assign them a meal or two to plan and prepare.

- **Choose a few recipes that you can cook in larger quantities,** such as casseroles, soups, and stews, so that you have leftovers for lunch or busy evenings.

- **Head to the grocery store with a list** created from the meals you are planning. Don't go unprepared, especially on an empty stomach; I always end up buying unintended items when I'm without a list and hungry at the grocery store!

- **Wash and pre-cut produce (when possible).** Some fruits and veggies do not hold up well if they are washed and cut ahead of time, but most do, like bell peppers (to keep them from getting slimy, wrap in a paper towel), broccoli, Brussels sprouts, cabbage, carrots, cauliflower, celery, cucumbers, green beans, leeks, onions, sweet potatoes, winter squash, and zucchini. I do not recommend pre-cutting okra, tomatoes, or white potatoes.

- **Have plenty of reusable storage containers,** as well as freezer-safe zip-top bags in many sizes and a Sharpie for labeling.

- **Prep as many vegetable and spice combinations for your planned meals as possible.** I pack the pre-cut veggies into gallon-size zip-top bags, and the spices into a smaller bag inside the large bag. I then label the outside of the gallon bag according to the recipe. When I teach a cooking class, this is how I manage several recipes in 90 minutes or less; almost all the ingredients are stored in one large bag!

- **Before starting a recipe, set out every ingredient and cooking tool you will need next to your workspace.** Cooking is a chore for some people because they keep having to run back and forth from stove to pantry. Collecting everything at once means less scurrying around. And if you have small children who are learning to cook, having them fetch the ingredients and tools is an ideal way to get them started.

- **Keep a running list of pantry items that need to be replaced.** I keep a whiteboard handy and snap a picture with my phone before I go shopping for an easy list that never gets lost at the store.

- **Enjoy the experience!** I like to listen to music or podcasts, watch a cooking show, or chat with my family while preparing meals. Sometimes I snack on cut-up veggies and a dip while I prep. Make this time relaxing and fun!

An estimated 25 percent or more of the produce we bring into our homes gets thrown out. The key to avoiding this fate for your fruits and vegetables is proper storage. Here are a few of my favorite storage strategies:

- These fruits and vegetables can be stored at room temperature until they are cut up: apples, avocados, bananas, citrus fruits (grapefruits, oranges, lemons, limes), mangoes, onions, papayas, pears, pineapples, pomegranates, potatoes, tomatoes, watermelons, and winter squashes (acorn, butternut, and pumpkin). But keep in mind that storing them in the refrigerator will slow the ripening process, which you may want to do if you have produce that is already ripe and ready to eat.

- Spread out your fruits and vegetables. The closer they are to each other, the quicker they will perish. And be sure to give your produce some air. Storing them in airtight plastic bags will suffocate them and speed up decay.

- Do not mix fruits and vegetables in the same bag. Fruits give off ethylene gas as they ripen, which can cause surrounding vegetables to perish more quickly. (*Tip:* Bananas produce an especially large amount of ethylene. If you have unripe produce, such as avocados, store them in a paper bag with a banana to ripen them up more quickly.)

- Mold spreads quickly and can ruin surrounding produce. Check for and discard rotten fruits and vegetables frequently. One bad apple can truly spoil the whole bunch!

- Wash and dry all leafy greens (I use a salad spinner, but you can also pat them dry) and then wrap them in a paper towel and place inside a loose plastic bag before storing in the refrigerator. Drying your leafy greens will prevent them from molding or rotting.

- Never wash mushrooms ahead of time; this will cause them to get slimy and degrade quickly. Store them in the refrigerator in their original containers.

Money-Saving Shopping Tips

Plant-based cooking doesn't have to be expensive! Try some of these strategies to save your grocery dollars:

- **Shop in the bulk section** for things like grains, nuts, nutritional yeast, flours, and dried beans. You can also purchase these kinds of ingredients in bulk on Amazon.

- **Snack on whole foods** like fruit, cut-up veggies and hummus, and popcorn rather than on expensive processed snack foods.

- **Always use dried beans.** It's worth your time to plan ahead and batch-cook your beans in a slow cooker or pressure cooker. Not only are dried beans sodium- and preservative-free, but they're budget friendly: they cost around $0.25/cup cooked, as opposed to $0.60/cup for canned beans. Store batch-cooked beans in small zip-top bags with 1½ cups of beans per bag, which is equivalent to the contents of a 15-ounce can of beans, a common unit in many recipes in this cookbook.

- **Buy frozen in addition to fresh veggies.** Buying vegetables in frozen form doesn't compromise their nutrient quality since vegetables are flash frozen soon after harvesting, and frozen veggies are often cheaper. Keeping some vegetables in your freezer also means you'll never be caught without something to prepare for dinner, even if you don't have time to get to the market.

- **Go homemade.** Packaged hummus, for example, is far more expensive than the homemade version, and usually contains oil and sodium. Making your own also means you can adjust the flavors, textures, and seasonings to exactly your preference.

- **Shop at your local farmers' market or join a CSA (Community Supported Agriculture).** Seasonal vegetables are always cheaper, as well as fresher!

A crucial step in building a PlantPure kitchen is tossing all the food items from your pantry that are not plant-based, as well as those that contain excessive oils, sugars, and salts. In order to do this, understanding how to read food labels is essential. Here are my tips for determining whether a product is worthy to sit on your shelves:

- Don't believe what is written on the front of the package; it is nothing more than a marketing pitch to sell a product. Phrases such as "all-natural" or "farm-fresh" are usually meaningless.

- Begin by reading the list of ingredients. These lists should be short and simple—when it comes to packaged food products, less is more.

  » Avoid all dairy products. Be on the look out for casein, whey, lactose, and milk solids in the ingredients list.

  » Ingredients are listed in descending order by weight, so you'll want to avoid products that list sugar as one of the first three ingredients and those that contain multiple sugars. Common names for types of sugars include high-fructose corn syrup, cane juice extract, evaporated cane juice, dextrose, fructose, galactose, glucose, maltose, sucrose, honey, lactose, liquid sugar, and molasses.

  » Seek out whole grains. Avoid white flour, wheat flour, enriched wheat flour, fortified wheat flour, and unbleached wheat flour.

  » Avoid all oils. That includes not only olive oil, soybean oil, canola oil, corn oil, and other familiar oils, but also butter, cocoa butter, coconut oil, hydrogenated fats and oils, partially hydrogenated fats and oils, lard, palm oil, shortening, monoglycerides, diglycerides, and lecithin.

- Check the nutrition facts panel for added sugars, salts, and oils and fat:

  » *Serving Size:* Be sure to adjust the sugar, fat, or sodium content for the serving size you actually eat. Often the suggested serving size listed on the package is unrealistically small.

» *Calories from Fat:* To find the percentage of total calories coming from fat, divide the calories from fat by the total calories. Generally, you want your diet as a whole to stay under 20 percent of calories from fat. Sometimes a whole food product (one without added oils) can exceed this number if it contains natural fats, such as avocado, soy, nuts, or seeds, and that is okay (see page 19 for an article by Dr. T. Colin Campbell on the fat in nuts). However, over the course of several days, you should be averaging no more than 20 percent of your calories from fat.

» *Sodium:* A handy way to calculate your recommended daily sodium intake is to take the number of calories you eat in a day and limit your sodium intake to no more than that same number in milligrams. So, for example, if you eat 1500 calories per day, your daily sodium intake should be less than 1500 milligrams.

Oh, Nuts!

T. Colin Campbell, PhD

Reprinted from the April 2016 issue of PlantPure Magazine.

In the whole food, plant-based food community, there is a tempest in the teapot and it's a pretty nutty tempest. By no means am I an expert on nuts—the foods, that is. My views on this topic are entirely based on the scientific research evidence, after professionally being in the field of nutrition for more than a half century.

So let's start with the evidence on nut consumption and human health. It's easy for me. I suggest reading Michael Greger's summary of the evidence in his new book, *How Not to Die* (2015).[1] It's the best recent review, in my opinion. Greger summarizes several studies of recent years that now suggest nuts are beneficial in reducing cardiovascular and other diseases. For women who are at high risk for heart disease, one study showed that those

who ate nuts five or more days a week cut their risk of a heart attack nearly in half compared to those eating one serving or less. Another long-term study of over 7,000 men and women at high risk for cardiovascular disease found that one group who doubled their intake of nuts to about an ounce (a handful) every day cut their risk of stroke in half. And in general, those in the study who ate more nuts every day "had a significantly lower risk of dying prematurely overall." Walnuts seem to have extra health benefits— those who ate more than three servings of walnuts a week cut their risk of dying from cancer in half.[2]

Nuts are one of the most nutrient dense of all plant-based foods. I recall many years ago teaching nutrition and pointing out that nuts are an especially good source of the fat-soluble antioxidant vitamin E. I imagined that this made sense because the purpose of nuts (and seeds) is to store the nutrients necessary for startup growth of the new tree offspring. My thought process at that time (probably not original) was that nuts might have to remain viable for long periods of time, until conditions become suitable for the nut to sprout new growth. This needs a good source of energy, and what better nutrient than fat, the most concentrated source. But, as I thought more about it, fats stored for many years might become rancid through oxidation of the fat, especially the more susceptible polyunsaturated fats. Nature solved this potential problem by adding a rich source of the antioxidant vitamin E (a group of antioxidant tocopherols and related isomers). And it chose the fat-soluble vitamin E, instead of the many water-soluble antioxidants found in other parts of the plant.

A second condition to be met for new growth is the inclusion of a rich supply of many other nutrients—vitamins and trace minerals. So, without belaboring the point, fat-soluble antioxidants such as vitamin E and unsaturated fats go together. So, too, do they work together in our bodies as well, and when we eat nuts, we are getting a good deal, including the addition of some interesting nut flavors to our culinary toolkit.

I know well the position of my colleague Dr. Caldwell Esselstyn and his enormously impressive accomplishments with his heart patients. He counsels these patients against the consumption of fatty foods, even those containing fats in their natural form, as in nuts and avocados. I have always felt it would be interesting to do a clinical trial, to see if the same or even more beneficial results could be obtained with a whole food, plant-based diet containing modest amounts of natural fats. But I understand the cautionary stance of Dr. Esselstyn. It is true that many nuts are sold in bags, already shelled, making them easy to over-consume. Eating too much of any rich food, even in whole form, may not be a good idea for people with heart disease.

But fat content aside, I am impressed with the findings now showing health benefits for most nuts. And when we

judge a food by one nutrient, in this case judging nuts only because of their fat content, we may be falling into the same trap that has caused so much past misinformation.

Investigating nutrients in isolation, i.e., reductionism, is fine when we are exploring the mechanisms by which they work. But for an understanding of a food's nutritional properties, we must seek and understand context, i.e., wholism. I am distressed by too much unnecessary confusion in this field called *nutrition*, most of which comes from interpretations based solely on reductionist research findings, a practice great for pharmaceutical firms and other financial interests.[3]

We should remember that the dairy industry argued for years that we should consume milk and cheese because these products contain calcium, which is important to bone health. This is a reductionist argument focused narrowly on consumption of calcium. As it turns out, foods high in animal protein such as cheese and milk cause a net calcium loss by causing a condition in the body called acidosis, which results in a leaching of calcium from the bones. So whatever calcium you take in when consuming milk or cheese is likely to be more than offset by the loss of calcium from the bones, excreted through the urine.

When we argue that nuts and avocados are unhealthy, we are using the same reductionist logic used by those promoting dairy consumption. And if we eliminate a whole category of foods abundantly available in most natural settings in temperate to tropical climates, a kind of food our ancestors would undoubtedly have found flavorful, then we are undermining the very rationale for a whole food, plant-based diet, which is rooted in Nature and in our evolution over eons. Even some of our primate cousins use stone tools to crack nuts, which they seem to relish. This is a story with deep roots.

I would never suggest people eat nuts and other fatty plant foods to excess, because these foods are not available in Nature in excessive amounts. These foods should be consumed in moderation, and if eaten this way, I believe they provide important beneficial health effects.

1. Greger, M. *How Not to Die*. 562 pp. (Flatiron Books, Inc., 2015).
2. Greger, *How Not to Die*, pp. 344–345.
3. See *Whole* for a more in-depth explanation of this argument: Campbell, TC. *Whole: Rethinking the Science of Nutrition*. 352 pp. (BenBella Books, 2014).

Dr. T. Colin Campbell *is the Jacob Gould Schurman Professor Emeritus of nutritional biochemistry at Cornell University and is best known for authoring the bestselling book* The China Study *with his son Thomas Campbell, M.D. He is the founder of the T. Colin Campbell Center for Nutrition Studies and the online Plant-Based Nutrition Certificate offered by the T. Colin Campbell Center for Nutrition Studies in partnership with eCornell. Dr. Campbell's expertise and scientific interests encompass relationships between diet and diseases, particularly the causation of cancer. He was trained at Cornell University (M.S., Ph.D.) and MIT (research associate) in nutrition, biochemistry, and toxicology, and has authored over 300 research papers. His legacy, the China Project, is the most comprehensive study of health and nutrition ever conducted.*

Breakfast

Don't Limit Yourself to "Breakfast Foods"

Have you ever wondered why sugary, processed cereals have become such a breakfast tradition? Originally, cereal was developed during the Industrial Revolution as Americans began leaving farms to work more sedentary jobs. Cereal could be consumed as a quick, light breakfast, and at first, these early products were reasonably healthful. But the sugary cereals lining the aisles today, with colorful, enticing packaging, are a far cry from the original Grape-Nuts and Corn Flakes developed over a hundred years ago.

What should you eat if you don't enjoy the healthier cereals? You don't have to restrict yourself to dry cereal, or oatmeal and fruit every day. Maybe you enjoy fruit as a snack, but not necessarily as a meal. Or perhaps you sometimes like a bowl of oatmeal and fruit as a light lunch. Don't be afraid to step outside the box. Eating a bowl of leftover chili, or brown rice with beans and a salad, is perfectly acceptable as a breakfast meal—and may even cut back on your grocery budget.

Should We Avoid or Limit Soy Products?

Including soy products as part of a whole food, plant-based diet is a highly debated topic. Many people avoid soy products because they contain phytoestrogens, which are believed to act like estrogens in the body. But some studies suggest that phytoestrogens actually decrease the effects of estrogen in the body, lowering the risk of breast, prostate, and other reproductive cancers.

Soy becomes a problem when we start consuming protein powders, excessive amounts of soy milk, processed soy-based energy bars, and fake meat products. Especially problematic is the soy protein isolate used in many processed foods.

But that doesn't mean there's no place in the whole food, plant-based diet for a moderate amount of tofu, tempeh, edamame, and miso. Just be sure to avoid genetically modified soy by purchasing organic (which ensures that the product does not contain GMOs).

Whether we're isolating the oil in olives or making high-fructose corn syrup from corn, the underlying problem is the same: The more we distance ourselves from the whole food, the more problems will likely appear. The bottom line is simple, for soy and all foods: For optimal health, eat plant-based foods in their whole form.

Chai Quinoa Porridge

This warm dish is a nice change from traditional oatmeal. I love the nutty flavor and texture of quinoa, and it's an excellent source of protein to get your day started right.

1 cup unsweetened plant-based milk

1 cup water

1 tablespoon pure maple syrup

¼ teaspoon pure vanilla extract

1 cup quinoa

½ cup raisins

½ teaspoon ground cinnamon

¼ teaspoon ground ginger

¼ teaspoon ground cloves

⅛ teaspoon ground cardamom

Toppings (optional)

Unsweetened coconut flakes

Chopped nuts

Fresh fruit

Yields: 2 servings
Prep Time: 10 minutes
Cook Time: 25 minutes

1. Combine all the ingredients (except the toppings) in a medium saucepan and bring to a boil over medium-high heat.

2. Reduce the heat to low, stir, and cook for 20 to 25 minutes, until the porridge is thick and the grains are tender. Continue to stir occasionally so the quinoa doesn't stick to the pan or burn. Add more water if you like your porridge thinner.

3. Serve with your favorite toppings.

Kim's Hint: *You can easily make this into oatmeal instead of quinoa porridge. Use the same amount of oats and prepare them according to the package instructions, adding the spices before cooking.*

Chia Seed Pudding

Chia seeds are loaded with beneficial nutrients and add a beautiful, thick texture to puddings and smoothies. I love making these pudding creations ahead of time in individual mason jars for a quick snack or meal. They're perfect for the work/school morning rush.

1 cup unsweetened plant-based milk

1 to 2 teaspoons pure maple syrup

¼ teaspoon pure vanilla extract

¼ cup chia seeds

1 tablespoon unsweetened coconut flakes

¼ teaspoon ground cinnamon

1 banana, sliced

½ cup fresh or frozen berries

Yields: 2 servings
Prep Time: 10 minutes, plus 1 hour to thicken
Cook Time: 0 minutes

1. In a small bowl, mix the milk, maple syrup, vanilla, chia seeds, coconut flakes, and cinnamon until the chia seeds are evenly dispersed.

2. Cover the bowl and refrigerate for at least 1 hour or overnight.

3. Serve topped with bananas and fresh berries.

Kim's Hint: *You can decrease the chia seeds to 2 tablespoons and add ¼ cup oats for a quick and easy oatmeal chia seed pudding.*

Mason Jar Oatmeal Breakfast

This tasty dish is perfect to make in the evening for a quick "grab and go" breakfast the next morning.

½ cup oats

1 cup unsweetened plant-based milk

1½ teaspoons pure maple syrup

¼ teaspoon pure vanilla or almond extract

½ cup blueberries

½ cup diced mango

1 to 2 tablespoons chopped walnuts

2 teaspoons chia seeds

Pinch of ground cinnamon

Yields: 1 serving
Prep Time: 10 minutes, plus overnight to chill
Cook Time: 0 minutes

Combine all the ingredients in a pint-size mason jar, cover, shake well, and refrigerate overnight. Eat it right out of the mason jar the next morning.

Kim's Hint: *Feel free to sub in your favorite berries, fresh fruit (bananas work great!), and nuts in this recipe to create your own flavor combination.*

Overnight Steel-Cut Oatmeal

Steel-cut oats have an exceptionally hearty, nutty flavor, but they can take a long time to cook—and let's face it, most of us are in a hurry on weekday mornings. This recipe lets you make steel-cut oats ahead of time with almost no effort. Serve with your favorite oatmeal toppings—we love sliced bananas, berries, dried fruit, chia seeds, and chopped nuts.

4 cups water

1 cup steel-cut oats

¼ teaspoon sea salt

Yields: 4 servings
Prep Time: 5 minutes, plus overnight to sit
Cook Time: 5 minutes

1. Bring the water to a boil in a medium saucepan over medium-high heat. When the water reaches the boiling point, stir in the oats and sea salt. Boil for about 1 minute. Remove from the heat and stir.

2. Cover the pot and let it sit overnight. There is no need to refrigerate.

3. In the morning, stir the oatmeal and rewarm over low heat for 3 to 5 minutes. Serve warm. Refrigerate leftovers for the next day.

Kim's Hint: You can make a double or even triple batch of this recipe if you want to have a week's worth of oatmeal on hand.

Pumpkin Porridge

I love pumpkin and the fall spices that go with it. If you're getting bored with classic oatmeal, this variation will give your breakfast a lift.

1 cup 100% pumpkin puree
(not pumpkin pie filling)

1 cup oats

1½ cups water

¼ cup raisins

½ teaspoon ground
cinnamon

¼ teaspoon ground nutmeg

¼ teaspoon ground ginger

⅛ teaspoon ground allspice

2 teaspoons pure maple
syrup (optional)

2 cups diced fresh fruit

2 tablespoons chopped nuts

Yields: 2 to 3 servings
Prep Time: 10 minutes
Cook Time: 10 minutes

1. Combine the pumpkin puree, oats, water, raisins, and spices in a medium saucepan and bring to a boil over medium heat. Reduce the heat to medium-low and cook for 5 to 10 minutes, until thickened.

2. Serve the porridge with the maple syrup (if desired), fresh fruit, and nuts.

Kim's Hints:

- *To make this recipe even simpler, you can replace all the spices with 1 rounded teaspoon of pumpkin pie spice.*
- *Feel free to use whatever fresh fruits you have on hand—bananas, mangoes, blueberries, and strawberries all taste great with this porridge.*

Almond or Cashew Milk

I recently started making our own plant-based milk and was pleasantly surprised at how easy it is to do. I purchased a reusable nut bag on Amazon, which makes straining a breeze. There are a variety of bags to choose from, but I strongly recommend a larger bag. If you are using a standard blender (that is, not a high-powered model like a Vitamix or NutriBullet), you'll need to soak your nuts in water overnight, then drain them. This milk tastes fresh and delicious and needs only a few ingredients.

1 cup raw almonds or
    cashews

4 cups water

2 tablespoons sweetener:
    pitted dates, pure maple
    syrup, or agave nectar
    (optional)

Pinch of sea salt

Yields: 4½ cups
Prep Time: 10 minutes
Cook Time: 0 minutes

1. Combine all the ingredients in a high-powered blender. Blend on high for 1 to 2 minutes, until completely smooth and creamy.

2. Strain the milk through a nut milk bag. This ensures that your milk will be smooth.

3. Store the milk in a covered glass container in the refrigerator for up to 3 days. Shake and serve cold.

Kim's Hint: *If you are using cashews, it may not be necessary to strain the milk as there will be a much smaller amount of nut pulp than with almond milk.*

Lemon Poppy Seed Pancakes

Our kids love lemon poppy seed muffins, so I created pancakes with the same flavor. You can find lemon extract and poppy seeds in the spice aisle of your supermarket. I love to serve these pancakes with fresh fruit or a warm blueberry sauce.

1½ cups unsweetened plant-based milk

1 tablespoon pure maple syrup

1 teaspoon pure vanilla extract

½ teaspoon lemon extract

1½ cups oat flour

2 teaspoons baking powder

1½ tablespoons poppy seeds

1 tablespoon grated lemon zest

¼ teaspoon ground ginger

Pinch of sea salt

Fresh fruit or fruit sauce, for serving (optional)

Yields: 4 servings
Prep Time: 10 minutes
Cook Time: 15 minutes

1. In a medium bowl, whisk together the milk, maple syrup, and vanilla and lemon extracts until smooth. Add the flour, baking powder, poppy seeds, lemon zest, ginger, and sea salt and stir until well combined. Allow the mixture to sit and thicken a bit. The batter should be thick but pourable. If it's too thin, add another tablespoon or two of flour. If it's too thick, add another tablespoon or two of milk.

2. Heat a nonstick griddle or skillet over medium heat. Pour about ¼ cup of batter per pancake onto the hot griddle and cook until the pancakes are bubbly on top and the edges are slightly dry, about 2 to 3 minutes. Turn and cook until the pancakes are browned on the other side, another 2 to 3 minutes or so. Repeat with the remaining batter. Serve with optional fresh fruit or fruit sauce.

Kim's Hint: *Feel free to substitute whole wheat flour or spelt flour for the oat flour.*

Blueberry Corn Cakes

Blueberry cornbread muffins are top on my list of delicious breads, but cornbread has to be eaten right out of the oven or it tends to dry out. That is why I came up with a recipe for corn cakes that never dry out—even though they are always eaten quickly in our house! Serve these with a fruit sauce for the perfect morning delight.

1 cup finely ground cornmeal

½ cup spelt flour

1 teaspoon baking powder

½ teaspoon baking soda

¼ teaspoon ground cinnamon

Pinch of sea salt

1½ cups unsweetened plant-based milk

1 tablespoon pure maple syrup

1 teaspoon pure vanilla extract

1 cup fresh or frozen blueberries

Fruit sauce, for serving (optional)

Yields: 4 servings
Prep Time: 10 minutes
Cook Time: 15 minutes

1. In a large bowl, whisk together the cornmeal, flour, baking powder, baking soda, cinnamon, and salt.

2. Add the milk, maple syrup, and vanilla and stir just until combined. Fold in the blueberries and let the batter sit for 5 minutes.

3. Heat a nonstick griddle or skillet over medium heat. Pour about ¼ cup of batter per pancake onto the hot griddle and cook until the pancakes are bubbly on top and the edges are slightly dry, about 2 to 3 minutes. Turn and cook until the pancakes are browned on the other side, another 2 to 3 minutes or so. Repeat with the remaining batter. Serve with optional fruit sauce.

Kim's Hint: Small frozen blueberries work best for this recipe.

Little Chickpea Omelets

I have always loved a good omelet. But when I stopped eating eggs, I discovered that I enjoy this chickpea version just as much! These are more like a light pancake, but you will be surprised how much they remind you of a fluffy, flavorful omelet.

Filling

4 ounces mushrooms, sliced

1 onion, diced

1 red bell pepper, seeded and sliced

10 ounces spinach, torn into bite-size pieces, or baby spinach

Sea salt

Black pepper

Omelet Batter

2 tablespoons flax meal or chia seeds

¼ cup water

¾ cup chickpea flour

2 tablespoons nutritional yeast flakes

¼ teaspoon baking powder

¼ teaspoon garlic powder

¼ teaspoon onion powder

¼ teaspoon ground turmeric

¼ teaspoon sea salt

⅛ teaspoon black pepper

¾ cup unsweetened plant-based milk

Toppings

1 cup salsa

1 avocado, pitted, peeled, and sliced

Yields: 4 servings
Prep Time: 10 minutes
Cook Time: 15 minutes

1. In a medium skillet over medium-high heat, sauté the mushrooms, onion, and red bell pepper in a small amount of water until tender, about 8 minutes. Add the spinach and cook briefly, just until wilted. Season with salt and black pepper to taste. Set the omelet filling aside.

2. In a small bowl, combine the flax meal and water and set aside until thickened.

3. In a medium bowl, whisk together the chickpea flour, nutritional yeast flakes, baking powder, garlic powder, onion powder, turmeric, salt, and black pepper.

4. Add the milk and the thickened flax mixture to the dry ingredients and mix until you have the consistency of pancake batter. If the batter is too thick, simply add a little more water.

5. Heat a nonstick griddle or skillet over medium heat. Pour about ¼ cup of the omelet batter onto the hot griddle for each pancake and cook until bubbly and dry around the edges, about 2 to 3 minutes. Flip and cook the other side for another 2 to 3 minutes.

6. Place one chickpea pancake on each plate. Spoon some of the vegetable mixture down the center of each chickpea pancake and fold it over the vegetables as you would with an omelet. Top with salsa and avocado slices and serve.

Morning Breakfast Potatoes

Potatoes are my favorite breakfast food. When I was a kid, my mother would often prepare eggs and potatoes as a special weekend breakfast. I quickly discovered that I preferred the potatoes because they were not just filling but loaded with savory flavors, like the perfectly balanced rosemary, garlic, and onion I use here.

4 medium red potatoes, cut into 1- to 2-inch cubes

1 small red onion, diced

½ red bell pepper, diced

1 tablespoon chopped fresh rosemary

1 teaspoon paprika

½ teaspoon garlic powder

½ teaspoon sea salt

¼ teaspoon black pepper

Yields: 4 to 6 servings
Prep Time: 15 minutes
Cook Time: 40 minutes

1. Preheat the oven to 425°F. Line a rimmed baking sheet with parchment paper.

2. In a gallon-size zip-top bag, combine all the ingredients and shake to evenly distribute the seasonings on the vegetables. Spread out the mixture in a single layer on the prepared baking sheet.

3. Bake for 30 to 40 minutes, tossing once halfway through, until golden and tender. Serve.

Kim's Hint: *I like to serve these with the Little Chickpea Omelets (page 41) and top them with a dash of Frank's Original Red Hot Sauce. If you have leftover potatoes, they make a great snack, or you can add them to a salad instead of croutons.*

Breads

Ancient Grains

What exactly are "ancient grains"? Are they more nutritious or better quality than regular grains, or is saying a grain is "ancient" just another way of tagging it as "organic"? Let's take a look.

Here's a list of the most common ancient grains:

Amaranth (gluten-free)
Chia (gluten-free)
Farro
Freekeh
Kamut
Millet (gluten-free)
Quinoa (gluten-free)
Sorghum (gluten-free)
Spelt
Teff (gluten-free)

All these grains are ancient forms of our modern grains, which have been genetically modified over time. For example, farro, freekeh, kamut, and spelt are all ancient varieties of modern-day wheat. Interestingly, some people who can't tolerate wheat because of a gluten sensitivity are able to enjoy these ancient grains.

The greatest benefit of ancient grains, however, is their higher nutrient value, which also results in a tastier, heartier flavor. Ancient grains are more likely to be grown organically, although you will still want to check product labels carefully.

Ancient grains can replace modern grains in any recipe, including bread, making it easy to take advantage of their benefits. Spelt is the most common alternative to modern wheat flour, and you may even find you prefer the taste and texture of homemade spelt bread to traditional wheat bread.

Blending and Baking:
Some Thoughts on Breads and Smoothies

Although not often mentioned in the same sentence, breads and smoothies are sometimes included in the same debate about processed foods and health. Both breads and smoothies can easily be made with whole foods and nutritious ingredients, and with no oil or added sugar. But while the ingredients may be wholesome, the way in which they are processed by the body is not quite as wholesome.

Our bodies process whole wheat bread differently than wheat berries. Because flours are highly processed or ground, they affect blood sugar and satiety cues differently than whole food. We can eat higher quantities more quickly and without the same sense of fullness. Similarly, we are less satiated by a smoothie than by two bananas, an apple, and a bunch of kale (the typical contents of one or two smoothie servings). Blended, processed, and condensed plant foods also elevate blood sugar more quickly than their whole food counterparts.

This isn't to say that breads and smoothies should be avoided entirely; sandwiches are extremely convenient when packing lunches, and smoothies can be a quick breakfast option. But looking at breads and smoothies as more occasional parts of our diet increases our opportunity for optimal health benefits.

Nutty No-Knead Spelt Bread

I love homemade bread, but I get impatient with all the kneading and rising. This bread is so simple to make—and much healthier than store-bought bread. If I know I'm going to be home for a few hours, I make multiple loaves. It requires almost no effort, just patience. I like to use spelt flour because it creates a slightly heavier texture than a typical whole wheat loaf, and it's very hearty and rustic.

2 cups lukewarm water

2 tablespoons pure maple syrup

1½ teaspoons active dry yeast

3 cups spelt flour

½ teaspoon sea salt

½ cup raisins

½ cup chopped walnuts

½ cup chopped pecans

¼ cup sunflower seeds

Yields: 6 to 8 servings
Prep Time: 10 minutes, plus 1 hour to rise
Cook Time: 45 minutes

1. In a small bowl, whisk together the water, maple syrup, and yeast. Let stand for 5 to 10 minutes.

2. In a large mixing bowl, mix the flour, salt, raisins, walnuts, pecans, and sunflower seeds until well combined. Add the wet ingredients to the dry ingredients and mix with a spoon. You should have a sticky dough at this point.

3. Line a loaf pan with parchment paper (or use a silicone loaf pan). Transfer the dough to the pan. Let the dough rest and double in size; this will take about 1 hour. When the dough is nearly done rising, preheat the oven to 350°F.

4. Bake the bread for about 45 minutes. The bread will be browned on top and will feel hollow when tapped. Remove the bread from the pan and place it on a cooling rack. Let it cool for 15 to 20 minutes before slicing.

> **Kim's Hint:** *I will put almost anything into this bread! You can add up to 2 cups of any dried fruit and nut combination that you prefer, or even granola.*

Rosemary Garlic Bread

My weakness is the Great Harvest Bread Company; I can't pass by that bakery without trying every sample they offer. My favorite bread is the rosemary herb, but it's made with white flour and that just won't work in our house. Here's my version: a delicious rosemary whole-grain bread. The secret is the fresh rosemary—I have tried it with dried rosemary, but it's never the same.

2 cups warm water

1½ tablespoons pure maple syrup

1½ teaspoons active dry yeast

3 cups whole wheat flour or spelt flour

3 tablespoons chopped fresh rosemary

2 tablespoons dried onion flakes

1½ teaspoons minced garlic

½ teaspoon sea salt

Yields: 6 to 8 servings
Prep Time: 10 minutes, plus 1 hour to rise
Cook Time: 45 minutes

1. Line a loaf pan with parchment paper (or use a silicone loaf pan) and set aside.

2. In a small bowl, whisk together the water, maple syrup, and yeast. Let stand for 5 to 10 minutes.

3. In a large mixing bowl, mix the flour, rosemary, onion flakes, garlic, and salt until well combined. Add the wet ingredients to the dry ingredients and mix with a spoon. You should have a sticky dough at this point.

4. Transfer the dough to the prepared loaf pan. Let the dough rest and double in size; this will take about 1 hour. When the dough is nearly done rising, preheat the oven to 350°F.

5. Bake for about 45 minutes. The bread will be browned on top and will feel hollow when tapped. Remove the bread from the pan and place it on a cooling rack. Cool for 15 to 20 minutes before slicing.

Cranberry-Orange Nut Bread

This bread is a staple at our Thanksgiving dinner table. I often turn the batter into muffins for a healthy breakfast on the go.

1 tablespoon flax meal or chia seeds

3 tablespoons water

2 cups whole wheat pastry flour

1½ teaspoons baking powder

½ teaspoon baking soda

¼ teaspoon sea salt

1 tablespoon grated orange zest

¾ cup orange juice

¼ cup unsweetened applesauce

¼ cup agave nectar or pure maple syrup

1 cup chopped fresh cranberries

½ cup chopped walnuts

Yields: 6 to 8 servings
Prep Time: 15 minutes
Cook Time: 1 hour

1. Preheat the oven to 375°F. Line a loaf pan with parchment paper.

2. In a small bowl, combine the flax meal and water. Set aside for 8 to 10 minutes to thicken.

3. In a large mixing bowl, whisk together the flour, baking powder, baking soda, salt, and orange zest.

4. In a separate bowl, combine the orange juice, applesauce, agave nectar, and thickened flax mixture. Add the wet ingredients to the dry ingredients and stir just until moistened. Do not overmix. Gently fold in the cranberries and walnuts.

5. Transfer the dough to the prepared pan. Bake until a knife inserted into the center comes out clean, 60 to 70 minutes. Remove the bread from the pan and place it on a cooling rack. Let it cool for 15 to 20 minutes before slicing.

Beer Bread

This bread has a unique nutty flavor that depends somewhat on the type of beer you choose. I love to serve this bread on a cold winter night with a hearty soup.

3 cups spelt flour

1 tablespoon baking powder

½ teaspoon sea salt

12 ounces beer (any variety, including nonalcoholic)

2 tablespoons pure maple syrup

Yields: 6 to 8 servings

Prep Time: 10 minutes

Cook Time: 1 hour

1. Preheat the oven to 375°F. Line a loaf pan with parchment paper (our use a silicone loaf pan).

2. In a large mixing bowl, whisk together the flour, baking powder, and salt.

3. Pour the beer and maple syrup into the dry mixture and stir until combined. The dough will be thick and sticky.

4. Transfer the dough to the prepared pan. You will need to spread it out a bit with your hands.

5. Bake for 1 hour. The bread will be golden brown on top and will feel hollow when tapped. Remove the bread from the pan and place it on a cooling rack. Let it cool for 15 to 20 minutes before slicing.

Pumpkin Raisin Yeast Bread

This is a hearty, dense yeast bread loaded with whole grains, nuts, raisins, and pumpkin. I love to toast a slice and slather it with apple butter.

1 cup lukewarm water

1 cup 100% pumpkin puree (not pumpkin pie filling)

¼ cup pure maple syrup

2 teaspoons active dry yeast

2¾ cups whole wheat flour or spelt flour

½ teaspoon sea salt

2 teaspoons pumpkin pie spice

1 cup raisins

½ cup chopped walnuts (optional)

Yields: 6 to 8 servings
Prep Time: 10 minutes, plus 1 hour to rise
Cook Time: 1 hour

1. Preheat the oven to 375°F. Line a loaf pan with parchment paper (or use a silicone loaf pan).

2. In a large mixing bowl, whisk together the water, pumpkin puree, maple syrup, and yeast until the ingredients are thoroughly combined and the yeast is dissolved.

3. Add the flour, sea salt, pumpkin pie spice, raisins, and walnuts (if using) and mix thoroughly. Transfer the dough to the prepared loaf pan and set aside to double in size, about 1 hour.

4. Bake for 45 minutes to 1 hour, until bread feels hollow when tapped. Remove the bread from the pan and place it on a cooling rack. Let it cool for 15 to 20 minutes before slicing.

Ginger Yeast Bread

I prefer this no-knead sweet bread to a traditional gingerbread cake. I especially enjoy it toasted, or made into French toast for breakfast.

2 cups lukewarm water

⅓ cup molasses

1½ teaspoons active dry yeast

3 cups spelt flour

1½ teaspoons ground ginger

1½ teaspoons ground cinnamon

1 teaspoon ground cloves

½ teaspoon sea salt

1 cup raisins

Yields: 6 servings
Prep Time: 10 minutes, plus 1 hour to rise
Cook Time: 45 minutes

1. Line a loaf pan with parchment paper (or use a silicone loaf pan).

2. In a small bowl, whisk together the water, molasses, and yeast. Let stand for 5 to 10 minutes.

3. In a large mixing bowl, mix the flour, ginger, cinnamon, cloves, sea salt, and raisins until well combined. Add the wet ingredients to the dry ingredients and mix with a spoon. You should have a sticky dough at this point.

4. Transfer the dough to the prepared loaf pan. Let the dough rest and double in size; this will take about 1 hour. When the dough is nearly done rising, preheat the oven to 350°F.

5. Bake for about 45 minutes. The bread will be golden brown on top and will feel hollow when tapped. Let the bread cool in the pan for 15 to 20 minutes. Remove the bread from the pan and place it on a cooling rack to cool completely before slicing.

Oatmeal Raisin Muffins

I love a big, fluffy muffin, but most made in bakeries today are loaded with oils and sugars. Here's my version of a healthier oatmeal raisin muffin! It's irresistible with a cup of hot tea.

1 tablespoon flax meal or chia seeds

3 tablespoons water

1½ cups whole wheat pastry flour

½ cup oats

2½ teaspoons baking powder

¼ teaspoon sea salt

½ teaspoon ground cinnamon

½ cup chopped walnuts

1 cup raisins

¾ cup unsweetened plant-based milk

½ cup unsweetened applesauce

¼ cup molasses

Yields: 8 to 10 muffins
Prep Time: 10 minutes
Cook Time: 25 minutes

1. Preheat the oven to 375°F. Line the cups of a muffin tin with silicone muffin molds (or use a nonstick muffin tin).

2. In a small bowl, mix the flax meal and water. Set aside for 8 to 10 minutes to thicken.

3. In a large mixing bowl, combine the flour, oats, baking powder, sea salt, cinnamon, walnuts, and raisins and mix thoroughly.

4. In a separate bowl, whisk together the milk, applesauce, molasses, and thickened flax mixture. Add the wet ingredients to the dry ingredients and mix only until moistened. Do not overmix the batter, as this will make your muffins tough.

5. Distribute the batter evenly among the muffin tin cups and bake for 20 to 25 minutes, until a toothpick inserted in the center of a muffin comes out clean. Remove from molds and allow to cool for 10 to 15 minutes before serving.

Strawberry Rhubarb Streusel Muffins

Rhubarb and strawberry season occur at the same time, so I'm always looking for different ways to enjoy them together. They give this muffin a very moist texture. I love to add spices to this particular recipe because it makes it even more exciting and delicious.

Streusel Topping

½ cup oats

5 small dates, pitted

¼ cup walnuts

½ teaspoon ground cinnamon

Batter

1 cup unsweetened plant-based milk

½ cup pure maple syrup

½ cup unsweetened applesauce

1 teaspoon apple cider vinegar

1 teaspoon pure vanilla extract

2¼ cups whole wheat pastry flour

2 teaspoons baking powder

½ teaspoon baking soda

¼ teaspoon sea salt

1 teaspoon ground cinnamon

½ teaspoon ground cardamom

1 cup finely chopped fresh rhubarb

1 cup chopped fresh strawberries

Yields: 10 to 12 muffins
Prep Time: 20 minutes
Cook Time: 25 minutes

1. Preheat the oven to 375°F. Line the cups of a muffin tin with silicone muffin molds (or use a nonstick muffin tin).

2. In a food processor, pulse the oats, dates, walnuts, and cinnamon until you have a crumbly texture. Do not overprocess. Set this aside for the streusel topping.

3. In a small bowl, whisk together the milk, maple syrup, applesauce, vinegar, and vanilla.

4. In a large mixing bowl, mix the flour, baking powder, baking soda, salt, cinnamon, cardamom, rhubarb, and strawberries until well mixed. Make sure the fruit is thoroughly coated with the flour mixture. Add the wet ingredients to the dry ingredients and mix until just combined. Do not overmix.

5. Distribute the batter evenly among the muffin tin cups and top each with the streusel mixture. Bake for 20 to 25 minutes, until a toothpick inserted in the center of a muffin comes out clean. Cool for 10 minutes before serving.

Burgers, Sandwiches, and Wraps

Plant-Based Lunch Boxes

Preparing a plant-based lunch to pack for work or school doesn't have to be stressful. Try some of these tips:

- **Keep it simple.** Stick with things you know everyone likes, and save experimentation with new foods for dinners and weekends. Keep a list of simple lunches, adding to it over time, and then rotate throughout the week.

- **Prep lunch components in advance.** That way you don't have to do it all every day. For example, prepare containers with all your sandwich components ahead of time. Then all you have to do in the morning is throw them together.

- **Think of your lunch box in three sections:**
  1. Main (sandwich, leftovers, or frozen entrée)
  2. Salad (steamed or raw veggies)
  3. Snacks (fresh fruit, hummus and whole-grain crackers, edamame, oil-free tortilla chips, dried fruit and nuts, etc.)

- **Get the right gear.** An insulated thermos is nice for keeping leftovers warm. A bento-style lunch box with compartments is also useful, so you don't have to keep track of (and worry about losing) individual containers.

- **Involve your kids in the process.** Whether they're helping you prep the night before or assisting with last-minute items in the morning, teaching your kids how to pack a lunch will give them a skill even a lot of adults don't have. By engaging your kids in the lunch-packing routine, you're teaching them good habits they'll carry throughout their lives. And, even more importantly, if they help plan and prepare it, they're more likely to eat it.

Veggie Burger Formula

I have made many different variations on the veggie burger, but I rarely write down the combinations. I have a tendency to use whatever vegetables are in season along with whatever else is available in my kitchen.

These are the seven categories of ingredients I almost always use when building a great burger. Get creative! You will find yourself coming up with some interesting combinations of flavors and textures.

Egg replacer: 1 tablespoon flax meal or chia seeds mixed with 3 tablespoons water and allowed to thicken

1 (15-ounce) can beans, rinsed and drained, or 1½ cups cooked beans: black beans, chickpeas, pinto beans, or cannellini beans

½ cup texture ingredients: chopped walnuts, olives, sundried tomatoes, cooked rice, cooked quinoa, or cooked bulgur wheat

1 cup dry base: oats, whole wheat or gluten-free bread crumbs, or crushed Rice Chex or Corn Chex cereal

2 cups finely chopped or shredded veggies: carrots, celery, spinach, kale, squash, sweet potato, or beets

3 tablespoons liquid flavor: mustard, ketchup (low sodium/sugar), soy sauce (low sodium), tamari (low sodium), vegan Worcestershire sauce, salsa, Buffalo sauce, balsamic vinegar, or any combination of the above

2 to 3 teaspoons seasoning: ground cumin, chili powder, Italian herb blend, garlic powder, curry powder, crushed fennel seeds, smoked paprika, black pepper, or any combination of the above

Yields: 4 to 6 burgers
Prep Time: 15 minutes
Cook Time: 25 minutes

1. Preheat the oven to 400°F. Line a baking sheet with parchment paper.

2. Mix your egg replacer and let it sit until thickened.

3. In a large mixing bowl, mash the beans with a potato masher (or pulse in a food processor). Do not puree. Add the egg replacer and the remaining ingredients and mix until thoroughly blended.

4. Form the mixture into 4 to 6 equal patties and place on the prepared baking sheet. Bake until golden brown and firm to the touch, 20 to 30 minutes. Flipping is not necessary. Serve with your desired accompaniments.

Beet Burgers

I love the color, flavor, and texture of these delicious plant-based burgers. I use only one beet because it adds enough color and texture without overpowering the flavor of the other ingredients. I also like to use red quinoa for a darker-colored burger.

2 tablespoons flax meal or chia seeds

6 tablespoons water

1 (15-ounce) can chickpeas, rinsed and drained, or 1½ cups cooked chickpeas

1 large beet, cooked, peeled, and cubed

2 carrots, peeled and quartered

1 tablespoon tahini

1 teaspoon garlic powder

1 teaspoon onion powder

½ cup cooked quinoa

¼ cup oats

½ teaspoon sea salt

Yields: 6 burgers
Prep Time: 15 minutes
Cook Time: 30 minutes

1. Preheat the oven to 375°F. Line a baking sheet with parchment paper.

2. In a small bowl, mix the flax meal and water. Set aside until thickened.

3. Transfer the thickened flax mixture to a food processor. Add all the remaining ingredients and process until you have a cookie dough–like consistency.

4. Using slightly wet hands, form the mixture into six equal patties. Place the patties on the prepared baking sheet.

5. Bake for 20 to 30 minutes, until dry to the touch. Serve.

Kim's Hint: *Many supermarkets offer cooked beets in the produce section or at the salad bar.*

Green Garden Burgers

These burgers are loaded with whole grains, greens, and flavor. The quinoa gives them a nice texture with a bit of crunch around the edges.

½ cup quinoa

1¼ cups water, divided

2 tablespoons flax meal or chia seeds

1 (15-ounce) can chickpeas, rinsed and drained, or 1½ cups cooked chickpeas

¼ cup oats

½ cup chopped red onion

3 garlic cloves, peeled

1 packed cup kale leaves (stems removed)

2 carrots, peeled and quartered

2 tablespoons tahini

3 tablespoons nutritional yeast flakes

½ teaspoon sea salt

4 to 6 whole wheat hamburger buns, toasted if desired

Plant-based mayonnaise

Sliced tomatoes

Sprouts

Yields: 4 to 6 burgers
Prep Time: 20 minutes
Cook Time: 35 minutes

1. Preheat the oven to 375°F. Line a baking sheet with parchment paper.

2. Combine the quinoa and 1 cup of the water in a small saucepan and bring to a boil over medium-high heat. Reduce the heat to low, cover the pan, and simmer until the quinoa is tender and fluffy, about 15 minutes.

3. Meanwhile, in a small bowl, mix the flax meal and the remaining ¼ cup water. Set aside to thicken.

4. Combine the chickpeas, oats, red onion, garlic, kale, and carrots in a food processor. Pulse until everything is finely chopped with no large chunks.

5. Transfer the mixture from the food processor to a large mixing bowl. Add the cooked quinoa, flax mixture, tahini, nutritional yeast, and salt. Mix until thoroughly blended.

6. Form the mixture into 4 to 6 equal patties and place them on the prepared baking sheet. Bake for 15 to 20 minutes, until golden around the edges.

7. Serve the burgers on the buns, topped with mayonnaise, sliced tomatoes, and sprouts.

Sweet Peanut Burgers

This quick, easy recipe is loaded with sweet and spicy Thai flavors. The combination of sweet potatoes and peanut butter gives these burgers a beautiful texture and taste.

1 tablespoon flax meal or chia seeds

2 tablespoons water

1 (15-ounce) can chickpeas, rinsed and drained, or 1½ cups cooked chickpeas

½ cup shredded sweet potatoes

¼ cup oats

3 tablespoons all-natural peanut butter (100% peanuts)

1 tablespoon lime juice

2 teaspoons rice vinegar

1 teaspoon low-sodium tamari

1 teaspoon sriracha

1 teaspoon grated fresh ginger

½ teaspoon garlic powder

¼ cup chopped fresh cilantro

Spicy Peanut Sauce

¼ cup all-natural peanut butter (100% peanuts)

3 tablespoons low-sodium tamari

1 tablespoon sriracha

1 tablespoon lime juice

2 teaspoons pure maple syrup

½ teaspoon garlic powder

Yields: 4 burgers
Prep Time: 20 minutes
Cook Time: 25 minutes

1. Preheat the oven to 375°F. Line a baking sheet with parchment paper.

2. In a small bowl, mix the flax meal and water. Set aside to thicken.

3. In a food processor, pulse the chickpeas. Do not turn the beans into a paste; just coarsely chop them. (You can also mash them with a fork.) Transfer the chickpeas to a large mixing bowl.

4. Add the flax mixture and all the remaining ingredients. Mix thoroughly with your hands. Form the mixture into four to six equal patties and place them on the prepared baking sheet.

5. Bake for 20 to 30 minutes, until golden brown.

6. While the burgers are cooking, whisk together all the sauce ingredients and set aside.

7. Top the burgers with the sauce and serve.

Carrot Dogs

When I first saw carrot dog recipes all over the web, done in a variety of ways, I thought it sounded very strange. But I'm an adventurist when it comes to plant-based foods, so I had to give it a try. Surprisingly, they're so good that even my omnivore friends love them! I am not sure where this idea originated, but many thanks to the creator.

4 large carrots

¼ cup apple cider vinegar

¼ cup water

2 tablespoons low-sodium tamari

1 teaspoon molasses

¼ teaspoon liquid smoke

¼ teaspoon garlic powder

¼ teaspoon onion powder

¼ teaspoon black pepper

4 whole-grain hot dog buns, toasted if desired

Toppings (optional)

Ketchup (low sodium/sugar)

Dijon mustard

Diced onion

Coleslaw

Sauerkraut

Relish

Chili

Yields: 4 servings
Prep Time: 15 minutes, plus overnight to marinate
Cook Time: 30 minutes

1. Peel the carrots, trim the ends, and cut them to the length of your hot dog buns.

2. Bring a medium saucepan of water to a boil over medium-high heat. Add the carrots and cook for 5 to 8 minutes, until tender but not mushy. Drain the carrots in a colander and put them under cold running water. This shocks them and prevents them from getting any softer.

3. In a small bowl, whisk together the vinegar, water, tamari, molasses, liquid smoke, garlic powder, onion powder, and pepper. Transfer the marinade to a large zip-top bag and add the cooled carrots. Toss gently to coat. Refrigerate overnight.

4. Preheat the oven to 400°F. Line a rimmed baking sheet with parchment paper.

5. Remove the carrots from the marinade and place on the prepared baking sheet. Bake for 15 to 20 minutes, until heated through and slightly browned.

6. Serve the carrots in the hot dog buns with your choice of toppings.

Teriyaki Tempeh Sandwiches

We love to visit popular pizza and sandwich chain Mellow Mushroom because they have delicious hoagies. Our favorite is their marinated tempeh or tofu hoagie with plenty of avocados, tomatoes, and sprouts. The marinated tempeh/tofu is so delicious that you hardly need any condiments to enjoy this sandwich; it's already bursting with flavor. Here's our family's attempt to create a homemade version using teriyaki sauce.

Marinade

¼ cup low-sodium tamari

¼ cup water

2 tablespoons pure maple syrup

1 teaspoon molasses

1 teaspoon red wine vinegar

½ teaspoon garlic powder

½ teaspoon ground ginger

Sandwiches

1 (8-ounce) package tempeh, thinly sliced

4 whole wheat sub rolls, toasted

1 or 2 avocados, pitted, peeled, and thinly sliced

1 tomato, thinly sliced

2 cups sprouts

Plant-based mayonnaise (optional)

Yields: 4 servings
Prep Time: 15 minutes, plus 2 hours to marinate
Cook Time: 25 minutes

1. In a medium bowl, whisk together all the marinade ingredients. Add the tempeh slices and toss to coat. Let them marinate for at least 2 hours. The longer they marinate, the better—I often let them marinate overnight in the refrigerator.

2. Preheat the oven to 400°F. Line a baking sheet with parchment paper.

3. Remove the tempeh from the marinade and place on the prepared baking sheet. Bake for 25 minutes.

4. Fill each sub roll with some of the tempeh and top with avocados, tomato slices, sprouts, and mayonnaise (if using). Serve warm.

Toasted Cheez Sandwiches

These are a sure-fire winner with children. To save time, try using frozen or leftover cooked sweet potatoes. You can whip up the cheese mixture in no time and store it for afternoon sandwiches.

1 medium sweet potato, peeled and diced

½ cup raw cashews

2 tablespoons nutritional yeast flakes

1 cup water

1 tablespoon Dijon mustard

2 teaspoons lemon juice

½ teaspoon onion powder

½ teaspoon garlic powder

Sea salt

4 slices whole wheat bread

1 large tomato, thinly sliced

Yields: 2 sandwiches
Prep Time: 15 minutes
Cook Time: 15 minutes

1. Put the diced sweet potato in a medium saucepan and cover with water. Cook over high heat until the water begins to boil. Reduce the heat to medium-low and simmer until the potatoes are softened, about 15 minutes. Drain and cool.

2. Transfer the sweet potatoes to a high-powered blender or food processor. Add the cashews, nutritional yeast, water, mustard, lemon juice, onion powder, garlic powder, and salt to taste. Blend until smooth. You may have to stop and scrape the sides a few times.

3. Heat a nonstick griddle or skillet over medium heat. Smear ¼ cup of the sweet potato cheez on two slices of the bread and top with a few tomato slices. Cover with the other two slices of bread. Place the sandwiches on the griddle and brown both sides. Serve warm.

Kim's Hints:

- *Save time by using ½ cup frozen mashed sweet potatoes.*
- *You can add any toppings you like to this sandwich. My favorite combination is sprouts, green olives, and roasted red peppers.*

Portobello Mushroom Sandwiches

Portobello mushrooms make a great meat alternative because they are slightly chewy and absorb flavor very well. They go perfectly with the sweet, vinegar-based dressing.

2 tablespoons balsamic vinegar

2 tablespoons low-sodium tamari

1 teaspoon pure maple syrup

1 teaspoon dried rosemary

½ teaspoon garlic powder

4 portobello mushroom caps

4 whole wheat hamburger buns, toasted if desired

4 thin tomato slices

4 thick red onion slices

2 avocados, pitted, peeled, and sliced

4 romaine lettuce leaves

Yields: 4 servings
Prep Time: 20 minutes
Cook Time: 20 minutes

1. In a large shallow dish, whisk together the vinegar, tamari, maple syrup, rosemary, and garlic powder. Put the mushroom caps in the bowl and toss so they are well coated. Let the mushrooms marinate for 15 to 20 minutes, turning occasionally and spooning the sauce over the mushrooms.

2. Preheat the oven to 400°F. Line a baking sheet with parchment paper.

3. Remove the mushrooms from the marinade and place them on the prepared baking sheet. Bake, turning once, for 15 to 20 minutes.

4. Serve the mushroom burgers on whole wheat buns with tomatoes, onions, avocados, and lettuce.

Kim's Hint: *I love serving these mushrooms with a tablespoon or two of Walnut Pesto (page 144) on the bun. It adds a fresh, creamy base for this sandwich.*

African Wraps

This recipe was inspired by the Creamy African Stew recipe in *The PlantPure Nation Cookbook*. That recipe was so popular that I was inspired to create a wrap with similar flavors. It is quick to make, bursting with great taste, and truly a winner.

2 large sweet potatoes, peeled and quartered, or 2 cups frozen sweet potato chunks

⅓ cup all-natural peanut butter (100% peanuts)

1 cup frozen corn, thawed

2 chipotle peppers in adobo sauce, minced

2 tablespoons adobo sauce

1 tablespoon grated fresh ginger

½ teaspoon ground cumin

4 to 6 whole wheat tortilla wraps

1 mango, pitted, peeled, and diced, or 1½ cups frozen (thawed) mango chunks

4 to 6 green onions, chopped

½ cup chopped fresh cilantro

2 cups fresh sprouts or mixed greens

Yields: 4 to 6 wraps
Prep Time: 15 minutes
Cook Time: 15 minutes

1. Put the sweet potatoes in a medium saucepan and cover with water. Cook over high heat until the water begins to boil. Reduce the heat to medium-low and simmer until the potatoes are tender when poked with a fork. Drain the sweet potatoes and transfer them to a medium bowl. Roughly mash the sweet potatoes.

2. Add the peanut butter, corn, chipotle peppers, adobo sauce, ginger, and cumin to the sweet potatoes. Mix gently until completely combined.

3. To serve, spread some of the sweet potato mixture onto each tortilla and top with some of the mango, green onions, cilantro, and sprouts, then roll them up.

Kim's Hint: *You can also use this filling for Raw Collard Wraps (page 80) if you prefer a gluten-free option.*

Raw Collard Wraps

This hardly feels like an actual recipe, but it was worth including because people are always surprised when I tell them that they can make wraps with collard greens. The key is to remove the toughest part of the stems and think of the leaf as a tortilla. These are easy, delicious, and fun to share. Did I mention they are gluten free?

4 to 6 large collard leaves

1 cup hummus (no added oils)

1 cup cooked quinoa or brown rice

1 cup shredded carrots

1 cup shredded red cabbage

1 cup sprouts

1 avocado, pitted, peeled, and sliced

1 red bell pepper, seeded and thinly sliced

½ cup salad dressing of your choice (see pages 83 to 92)

Yields: 4 to 6 wraps
Prep Time: 10 minutes
Cook Time: 0 minutes

1. Wash the collard leaves and remove the tough stalks on the ends. I usually remove the stem from the bottom to about halfway through the leaf. It will be difficult to roll these if you remove the entire stem.

2. Optional step: Bring a medium saucepan of water to a boil over medium-high heat. Using tongs, briefly put each collard leaf into the boiling water until bright green, and then remove. Transfer to a colander and shock under cold running water. Pat them dry with paper towels.

3. Lay out the collard leaves and spread each with some hummus. Top them with some quinoa, vegetables, and dressing. Fold the sides over and roll them up like a burrito. Slice in half crosswise and serve.

Kim's Hints:

- *You can absolutely skip step 2, but blanching the collard leaves will make them bright green and tender.*
- *Feel free to load up your collard greens with whatever filling you enjoy. I especially like to use the filling from the African Wraps (page 79).*

Dressings and Sauces

Swapping the Salt

It's a common misconception that less salt equals less flavor. With the right seasonings, it's possible to increase flavor without adding any salt at all. Instead of automatically salting your meal, try these flavor enhancers (alone or in combination) during cooking or at serving time:

- Vinegar: Vinegar provides more depth of flavor than salt and is available in endless varieties. Balsamic vinegars alone come infused with flavors such as fig, pomegranate, lemon, and black walnut. Rice vinegars also come with various flavor infusions (just be sure to check for added sugars). If you can't find specialty vinegars at your local grocery store, try Amazon or any gourmet food website.

- Garlic

- Black or cayenne (red) pepper

- Fresh lemon or lime juice

- Nutritional yeast

In addition to these ideas, you can try one of the many salt-free seasoning combinations on the market. Benson's Table Tasty is a popular salt replacer made from dehydrated lemon peel. Mrs. Dash makes excellent salt-free blends, available in most supermarkets nationwide. Just be sure to read the ingredients of any salt-free seasoning to make sure there is no added sodium from other sources.

Finally, if you do use salt, always add it just before serving. Season early, salt last!

How to Store Your Dressings and Sauces

While you can store your dips and spreads in Tupperware-style containers, dressings and sauces are easier to store in salad dressing bottles, which also makes drizzling them over your salad that much easier. You can find inexpensive salad dressing bottles on Amazon or at any kitchen store, but if you want to use something already in your kitchen, try mason jars or recycled glass dressing bottles.

I recommend using homemade dressings and sauces within a week, as they are not nearly as fresh and flavorful beyond that point. It's better to make small batches and use them often.

Cilantro-Lime Dressing

This fresh dressing is perfect on any hearty Mexican salad. It's sweet and creamy, with the perfect amount of spice.

1 large ripe avocado, pitted and peeled

2 garlic cloves, peeled

1 jalapeño, seeded

½ cup fresh cilantro leaves (loosely packed)

½ cup orange juice

¼ cup water, or more as needed

2 tablespoons lime juice

2 tablespoons apple cider vinegar

1 tablespoon pure maple syrup

¼ teaspoon ground cumin

¼ teaspoon sea salt

Yields: 1¼ cups
Prep Time: 10 minutes
Cook Time: 0 minutes

Combine all the ingredients in a blender or food processor and blend until creamy. If you prefer a thinner consistency, add more water, a tablespoon at a time. Store in an airtight container in the refrigerator for up to 5 days.

Blue Cheez Dressing

This recipe is also in *The PlantPure Nation Cookbook*, but that version requires a sub-recipe of Tofu-Cashew Mayonnaise. I've simplified it here by incorporating the ingredients from the mayonnaise into the recipe. The secret ingredient that makes this so close to a real blue cheese dressing is the tahini, for the uniquely sharp flavor of blue cheese. Our family and friends love this recipe!

2 tablespoons raw cashews

4 ounces extra-firm tofu

1 garlic clove, peeled

3 tablespoons lemon juice

3 tablespoons apple cider vinegar

2 tablespoons tahini

1 tablespoon water

2 teaspoons agave nectar or pure maple syrup

1½ teaspoons Dijon mustard

¾ teaspoon white vinegar

½ teaspoon sea salt

Toppings

2 tablespoons finely chopped green onions or fresh parsley

¼ cup crumbled extra-firm tofu

Yields: ¾ cup
Prep Time: 15 minutes
Cook Time: 0 minutes

Combine all the ingredients (except the toppings) in a high-powered blender. Blend until smooth and creamy. Fold in the green onions and crumbled tofu. Store in an airtight container in the refrigerator for up to a week.

Caesar Dressing

A typical Caesar dressing calls for anchovies, which impart a slightly fishy flavor. I use seaweed instead, but if you don't like seaweed, simply leave it out and sub in fresh parsley or chives. You can find a similar recipe in *The PlantPure Nation Cookbook*, but this is an easier version since there is no sub-recipe for the Tofu-Cashew Mayonnaise.

2 tablespoons raw cashews

4 ounces extra-firm tofu

⅓ to ½ nori sheet, torn into small pieces

½ cup water

2 tablespoons apple cider vinegar

1 tablespoon low-sodium tamari

2 teaspoons lemon juice

2 teaspoons Dijon mustard

2 teaspoons pure maple syrup

1 teaspoon nutritional yeast flakes

1 teaspoon garlic powder

Yields: 1¼ cups
Prep Time: 10 minutes
Cook Time: 0 minutes

Combine all the ingredients in a high-powered blender and process until smooth. Store in an airtight container in the refrigerator for up to a week.

Creamy Mustard Dressing

I love honey mustard dressings because they are creamy and full of sweet flavors. This recipe uses cashews and dates instead of honey for that perfect creamy sweetness.

½ cup raw cashews

5 Medjool dates, pitted, or ¼ cup pure maple syrup

1 cup water

¼ cup Dijon mustard

2 tablespoons apple cider vinegar

1 tablespoon lemon juice

¼ teaspoon sea salt

Yields: 1¾ cups
Prep Time: 10 minutes
Cook Time: 0 minutes

Combine all the ingredients in a high-powered blender and blend until smooth and creamy. Store in an airtight container in the refrigerator for up to a week.

Creamy Ranch Dressing

You will never miss dairy-based ranch after you try this recipe.

2 tablespoons raw cashews

4 ounces extra-firm tofu

2 garlic cloves, peeled

½ cup water

2 tablespoons apple cider vinegar

1 tablespoon lemon juice

2 teaspoons Dijon mustard

1 teaspoon pure maple syrup

2 teaspoons dried parsley

1 teaspoon dried dill

½ teaspoon onion powder

¼ teaspoon sea salt

½ teaspoon black pepper

Yields: 1¼ cups
Prep Time: 10 minutes
Cook Time: 0 minutes

Combine all the ingredients in a high-powered blender and blend until smooth and creamy. Store in an airtight container in the refrigerator for up to a week.

Carrot Ginger Dressing

I love the taste and texture of the creamy ginger dressings that most Japanese restaurants serve with their salads. However, they often have traditional mayonnaise in the recipe. This healthy plant-based version is just as delicious and even more flavorful than any I've had before.

2 carrots, peeled and quartered

½ onion

2 teaspoons grated fresh ginger

½ cup rice vinegar

2 tablespoons pure maple syrup

1 tablespoon miso

1 tablespoon tahini

½ teaspoon garlic powder

Yields: about 1 cup
Prep Time: 10 minutes
Cook Time: 0 minutes

Combine all the ingredients in a high-powered blender and blend on high until smooth. If you prefer this dressing slightly grainy, you can stop blending when you feel the texture is just right for you. Store in an airtight container in the refrigerator for up to a week.

Orange Tahini Dressing

Use this dressing for any salad or as a sauce for any stir-fry vegetable combination. It's also perfect for marinating tofu or tempeh slices. I like to marinate the tofu or tempeh for at least 1 hour (or overnight for best results) and then bake it at 400°F until browned and crispy around the edges.

¼ cup orange juice

¼ cup water

1 tablespoon lime juice

1 tablespoon lemon juice

1 tablespoon low-sodium tamari

1 tablespoon tahini

1 teaspoon pure maple syrup

1 teaspoon sriracha

3 garlic cloves, peeled

Yields: ¾ cup
Prep Time: 5 minutes
Cook Time: 0 minutes

Combine all the ingredients in a blender and blend until smooth. Store in an airtight container in the refrigerator for up to a week.

Kim's Hint: *I like to use a blender for this recipe rather than whisking by hand because it helps emulsify the ingredients.*

Thai Dressing

This is a wonderful dressing for any chopped or Asian salad. Creamy and full of flavor, it also makes the perfect topping for a veggie burger.

¼ cup raw cashews

½ cup unsweetened plant-based milk

¼ cup water

2 tablespoons canned lite coconut milk

1½ tablespoons apple cider vinegar

1 tablespoon green curry paste

1 tablespoon lime juice

1 tablespoon low-sodium tamari

1 teaspoon pure maple syrup

5 large fresh basil leaves

Yields: 1¼ cups
Prep Time: 10 minutes
Cook Time: 0 minutes

Combine all the ingredients in a blender and blend on high until smooth and creamy. Store in an airtight container in the refrigerator for up to a week.

Kim's Hint: *My favorite brand of oil-free green curry paste is Thai Kitchen.*

Tofu-Cashew Mayonnaise

This plant-based mayonnaise is so rich and full of flavor that you will not miss your old egg- and oil-based mayonnaise. This entire recipe only uses ¼ cup of raw cashews, which makes it lower in fat than commercially prepared vegan mayonnaises. I like to make a batch every week or two to have on hand—consider it part of your pantry! I use this mayonnaise for sandwiches, dressings, and sauces.

¼ cup raw cashews, soaked in water to cover for 2–3 hours, then drained

7 ounces extra-firm tofu

1/2 teaspoon sea salt

1/2 teaspoon tahini

4 teaspoons lemon juice

1½ teaspoons white vinegar

1 tablespoon Dijon mustard

2 tablespoons apple cider vinegar

2½ teaspoons agave nectar

2 tablespoons water

¼ teaspoon xanthan gum

Yields: 2 cups
Prep Time: 10 minutes
Cook Time: 0 minutes

1. Soaking the cashews in water for a few hours will reduce blending time. If you are not using a Vitamix, I highly recommend soaking the cashews so they blend into a smooth and creamy texture.

2. Put all the ingredients in a high-powered blender. Blend until smooth and shiny.

Kim's Hint: *If you do not have xanthan gum available you can skip this ingredient but the mayonnaise might have a slightly thinner consistency.*

Nut-Free Mayonnaise

The mayonnaise recipe I included in *The PlantPure Nation Cookbook* used tofu and cashews to replace mayonnaise's typical eggs and oil. A few people with nut allergies requested a mayonnaise without nuts, so this one uses coconut milk instead of cashews. Like cashews, coconut milk contains natural fats that help emulsify the ingredients. You won't miss egg-based mayonnaise with this recipe on hand!

7 ounces extra-firm tofu

¼ cup canned lite coconut milk

2 tablespoons apple cider vinegar

4 teaspoons lemon juice

1 tablespoon tahini

1 tablespoon Dijon mustard

1½ teaspoons white vinegar

1 teaspoon pure maple syrup

½ teaspoon sea salt

Yields: 1½ cups
Prep Time: 10 minutes
Cook Time: 0 minutes

Combine all the ingredients in a high-powered blender and blend until smooth and shiny. Store in an airtight container in the refrigerator for up to a week.

Creamy Horseradish Sauce

This mild sauce is great for veggie burgers, falafel, or zucchini cakes. It is slightly thinner than a traditional mayonnaise, which makes for a perfect drizzle.

4 ounces extra-firm tofu

2½ tablespoons prepared horseradish

2 tablespoons lemon juice

2 teaspoons apple cider vinegar

1 teaspoon pure maple syrup

½ teaspoon Dijon mustard

¼ teaspoon tahini

½ teaspoon dried dill

¼ teaspoon sea salt

¼ teaspoon black pepper

Yields: ¾ cup
Prep Time: 10 minutes
Cook Time: 0 minutes

Combine all the ingredients in a food processor or blender and process until smooth. Store in an airtight container in the refrigerator for up to a week.

Enchilada Sauce

Most canned enchilada sauces contain high amounts of sodium and added oils. This recipe has all the flavors of a traditional Mexican enchilada sauce without the unhealthy additives.

1 (28-ounce) can crushed tomatoes

2 Medjool dates, pitted

1 tablespoon lime juice

3 tablespoons whole wheat flour

2 tablespoons chili powder

1 teaspoon ground cumin

1 teaspoon dried oregano

1 teaspoon garlic powder

1 teaspoon onion powder

½ teaspoon smoked paprika

½ teaspoon sea salt

¼ teaspoon black pepper

Yields: 4 cups
Prep Time: 5 minutes
Cook Time: 10 minutes

1. Combine all the ingredients in a blender and blend until smooth.

2. Transfer the sauce to a medium saucepan. Cook over medium-high heat, stirring continuously, until bubbly. Turn the heat to low and continue to simmer until thickened, 5 to 10 minutes. Cool to room temperature, then store in an airtight container in the refrigerator for up to 2 weeks.

Hoisin Sauce

Hoisin is an Asian barbecue sauce that is used to flavor and season many Asian dishes. I like to make my own since it's cheaper and the ingredients are simple to find. This condiment is very salty and sweet, so a little can really go far; most recipes call for only a small amount of hoisin sauce to enhance the dish.

3 tablespoons low-sodium tamari

2 tablespoons all-natural peanut butter (100% peanuts)

2 tablespoons pure maple syrup

1 tablespoon molasses

1 tablespoon white vinegar

1 teaspoon sriracha

½ teaspoon garlic powder

½ teaspoon onion powder

¼ teaspoon Chinese five-spice powder

⅛ teaspoon black pepper

Yields: about ½ cup
Prep Time: 10 minutes
Cook Time: 0 minutes

Combine all the ingredients in a bowl and whisk until everything is well incorporated. Store in an airtight container in the refrigerator for up to a week.

Kim's Hint: *You can also use a blender for this recipe, but since the amounts are so small it's easier to use a hand whisk.*

Hollandaise Sauce

A typical hollandaise sauce is heavy with egg yolks and butter. This mild and creamy cashew-based version pairs nicely with almost any vegetable. We love to have it over asparagus with toast or polenta.

½ cup raw cashews

1 garlic clove, peeled

½ cup water

2 tablespoons lemon juice

2 teaspoons Dijon mustard

1 tablespoon nutritional yeast flakes

¼ teaspoon ground turmeric

Sea salt to taste

Yields: 1 cup or 4 servings
Prep Time: 10 minutes
Cook Time: 0 minutes

Combine all the ingredients in a high-powered blender and blend until smooth and creamy. Store in an airtight container in the refrigerator for up to a week.

Sweet BBQ Sauce

This sauce is wonderful for a stir-fry. I like to sauté broccoli, bell peppers, and carrots in a small amount of water until just tender and bright, then add this sauce for a tasty dinner. You can also use it marinate tofu, tempeh, Soy Curls, or jackfruit.

1 small onion, finely chopped

1 jalapeño, seeded and minced

4 garlic cloves, minced

1 cup water

¾ cup tomato paste

3 tablespoons apple cider vinegar

3 tablespoons pure maple syrup

2 tablespoons molasses

2 tablespoons vegan Worcestershire sauce

1 tablespoon low-sodium tamari

2 teaspoons smoked paprika

1 teaspoon cornstarch

Yields: 2¼ cups
Prep Time: 10 minutes
Cook Time: 10 minutes

1. In a small saucepan over medium-high heat, sauté the onion, jalapeño, and garlic in a small amount of water until tender, about 5 minutes.

2. In a small bowl, whisk together the remaining ingredients until well blended. Add the sauce to the pan, reduce the heat to medium, and stir the mixture continuously until bubbly and thickened, about 5 minutes. Cool to room temperature, then store in an airtight container in the refrigerator for up to a week.

Salads

Local, Organic, or Both?

Many of us spend Saturday morning or Sunday afternoon shopping at our local farmers' markets, where we are often faced with the decision of whether to buy local or organic produce. Of course, the best option is locally grown organic produce. But while some of the local produce found at farmers' markets is certified organic, much of it isn't. So what should you do? Are you better off buying organic carrots at the grocery store, shipped in from a distance, or buying local, noncertified organic at the farmers' market?

First, it's important to understand the costs of organic certification for growers. The initial certification can range anywhere from "a few hundred to several thousand dollars," according to the USDA. This cost does not include routine inspections, recertification, and all the time spent throughout the certification process.

Farms that earn revenue below a certain threshold can legally advertise their produce as organic without going through this process. But farms that bring in just enough revenue to fall outside this box often don't go through the certification process because they just can't justify the cost of USDA certification.

So the answer to the commonly asked question "Should I go local or organic?" is, first, get to know your farmers, otherwise known as "face certification." Ask if they use pesticides, and if so, what types and how much. Pick their brains about their farming methods. Farming is hard work, and so people are generally in it because they love what they do; they're generally happy to talk with you about their products and growing methods.

If you find that a local farm's methods aren't 100 percent organic but close to it, you should consider buying from the

farmer even if organic is important to you, especially considering that locally grown produce is picked at peak ripeness and so has more health-enhancing nutrients.

Also worth considering when deciding whether local or organic is more important: whether the product you're shopping for is on the "dirty dozen" or "clean fifteen" lists put out by the Environmental Working Group each year. The dirty dozen list includes items that typically have more pesticide residue, whereas the clean fifteen contain much less, due to factors like thicker peels or being grown underground.

2016 Dirty Dozen	2016 Clean Fifteen
apples	avocados
nectarines	corn
strawberries	pineapples
peaches	cabbage
blueberries	sweet peas
cherries	onions
grapes	asparagus
celery	mangoes
bell peppers	papayas
cucumbers	kiwi
cherry tomatoes	eggplant
spinach	honeydew
	grapefruit
	cantaloupe
	cauliflower

Weekend Veggie Prep

Don't wait until the workweek hits to prep your veggies! Reserve an hour or two on a Saturday or Sunday afternoon and devote that time to cutting, chopping, and stocking your fridge. You should plan on prepping for three categories: recipes, salads, and snacks. Recipe prep will be based on your meal plan for the upcoming week, and the rest will be more of a salad bar in your fridge. This way, whether you're having a salad for a snack or packing a lunch for work, all you have to do is pull out your containers and throw it together. You will find that spending a few hours in the kitchen on a weekend is a fair trade for a week's worth of convenience!

Artichoke and White Bean Salad

This salad can serve as a dip or sandwich/wrap filling. The artichokes, white beans, and olives (my favorites) give this dish the perfect texture.

1 (15-ounce) can cannellini beans, rinsed and drained, or 1½ cups cooked white beans

1 cup chopped canned artichokes, drained and rinsed

½ cup sliced or chopped black olives

2 celery stalks, diced

3 green onions, sliced

½ cup Tofu-Cashew Mayonnaise (page 94) or Nut-Free Mayonnaise (page 95)

1 tablespoon Dijon mustard

1 tablespoon nutritional yeast flakes

2 teaspoons dried rosemary

½ teaspoon garlic powder

¼ teaspoon black pepper

Sea salt to taste

Yields: 4 servings
Prep Time: 15 minutes
Cook Time: 0 minutes

In a large mixing bowl, mash the beans coarsely with a fork or potato masher. You don't want to puree the beans, so leave some small chunks remaining. Add the remaining ingredients and gently fold them together until everything is well combined. Serve.

Asian Coleslaw

This dish is a nice alternative to a traditional mayonnaise-based coleslaw. It has a wonderful mixture of flavors from the peanuts, lime, and ginger and is a perfect picnic-style dish to pass.

Dressing

¼ cup rice vinegar

¼ cup water

3 tablespoons low-sodium tamari

2 tablespoons pure maple syrup

2 tablespoons lime juice

1 to 2 teaspoons sriracha

½ cup all-natural peanut butter (100% peanuts)

2 teaspoons grated fresh ginger

1 teaspoon garlic powder

Vegetables

4 cups thinly sliced green cabbage

3 cups thinly sliced red cabbage

1 red bell pepper, seeded and thinly sliced

6 green onions, thinly sliced

2 carrots, peeled and julienned

1 cup frozen edamame or peas, thawed

1 cup canned or cooked chickpeas, rinsed and drained

½ cup chopped fresh cilantro

¼ cup chopped peanuts, for garnish

Yields: 6 servings
Prep Time: 20 minutes
Cook Time: 0 minutes

1. Combine all the dressing ingredients in a blender and blend until creamy.

2. Combine all the vegetables in a large bowl. Toss with the dressing until well blended. Garnish with the chopped peanuts and serve.

Asian Noodle Salad

This salad is a meal all by itself. The dressing is almost identical to the Asian Coleslaw (page 104) but with different vegetables and a starch base. I never hesitate to try different veggies in the mix depending on the season and what's in my fridge. The dressing makes this salad extra special.

Dressing

3 tablespoons lime juice

2 tablespoons low-sodium tamari

2 tablespoons water

1 tablespoon rice vinegar

1 tablespoon pure maple syrup

1 to 2 teaspoons sriracha

¼ cup all-natural peanut butter (100% peanuts)

2 garlic cloves, peeled

1 teaspoon grated fresh ginger

Noodles and Vegetables

8 ounces whole-grain soba noodles

2 cups thinly sliced red cabbage

2 cups shredded carrots

1 cup finely chopped kale

1 red bell pepper, seeded and thinly sliced

2 celery stalks, thinly sliced

4 green onions, thinly sliced

¼ cup chopped fresh cilantro

1 cup frozen edamame or peas, thawed

1 tablespoon sesame seeds, for garnish

Yields: 4 to 6 servings
Prep Time: 30 minutes
Cook Time: 12 minutes

1. Combine all the dressing ingredients in a blender and blend until creamy. Set aside. (It may thicken a bit as it sits.)

2. Cook the soba noodles according to the package instructions and rinse in a colander with cold water.

3. Combine all the vegetables in a large bowl and toss to combine. Add the noodles and dressing and toss thoroughly. Garnish with the sesame seeds and serve.

Kim's Hint: *This recipe makes a beautiful filling for a brown rice spring roll. Simply fill a romaine lettuce leaf with a scoop of the salad and wrap it burrito-style with a wet spring roll wrapper.*

Avocado-Mango Salad

This salad is the perfect addition to any Mexican dinner, such as tacos, enchiladas, or chili bowls. The tropical flavors of mango and lime are a perfect balance with the corn and avocado. This is a family favorite in the Campbell house.

1 tablespoon lime juice

1 tablespoon white balsamic vinegar

2 ripe mangoes, pitted, peeled, and diced

2 avocados, pitted, peeled, and cubed

1 cup corn, fresh or frozen (thawed)

½ red onion, finely diced

Sea salt

Black pepper

Yields: 4 servings
Prep Time: 15 minutes
Cook Time: 0 minutes

1. In a small bowl, whisk together the lime juice and balsamic vinegar.

2. In a large bowl, toss together the mangoes, avocados, corn, and onion. Coat with the lime juice mixture. Season with salt and pepper to taste and serve.

Kim's Hint: *This salad can easily be converted into a main dish by adding a cup or two of black beans along with a cup of cooked quinoa. Red quinoa complements the colors of this dish beautifully.*

Kale Power Salad

I love salads that feel like a meal all on their own! This salad is a powerhouse packed with all kinds of nutrients, flavors, and textures.

5 to 6 cups chopped kale

1 recipe Orange Tahini Dressing (page 91)

1 red bell pepper, seeded and diced

1 carrot, peeled and shredded

1 cup thinly sliced red cabbage

1 cup frozen edamame or peas, thawed

2 cups cooked quinoa

1 orange, peeled and sliced

¼ cup slivered almonds

Yields: 4 servings
Prep Time: 25 minutes
Cook Time: 0 minutes

Put the kale in a large bowl and drizzle the dressing over it. Use your hands to firmly massage the dressing into the leaves. The leaves will soften and wilt as you do this. I recommend massaging the leaves for 3 to 5 minutes to tenderize them. Add the remaining ingredients and toss well. Serve.

Kim's Hint: *There are countless other ingredients you can add or substitute in this salad. I sometimes use sliced strawberries and dried fruit, along with sunflower seeds or hemp seeds.*

Black Rice Salad with Garden Vegetables

Black rice, also known as forbidden rice, is rich in nutrients and fiber. It has a mild nutty flavor and turns a deep purple when cooked. You can certainly substitute brown rice or a rice blend for the black rice, but I like the chewy texture that black rice adds to a salad. The colorful vegetables combined with the deep purple rice make this a beautiful salad!

1 cup black rice

2 cups water

3 tablespoons orange juice

2 tablespoons Dijon mustard

2 tablespoons rice vinegar

1 tablespoon tahini

1 tablespoon sriracha

1 tablespoon low-sodium tamari

1 teaspoon grated fresh ginger

2 cups peas, fresh or frozen (thawed)

1 cup thinly sliced purple cabbage

3 carrots, peeled and shredded

1 red bell pepper, seeded and diced

3 green onions, sliced

1 (15-ounce) can chickpeas, rinsed and drained, or 1½ cups cooked chickpeas

¼ cup raw pistachios or pumpkin seeds, for garnish

Yields: 4 to 6 servings
Prep Time: 20 minutes
Cook Time: 1 hour

1. Rinse the rice well and put it in a small saucepan. Add the water and bring to a boil over medium-high heat. Reduce the heat to low, cover, and cook for 45 to 60 minutes, until the rice is tender and slightly chewy. Drain well and let cool.

2. In a small bowl, whisk together the orange juice, Dijon mustard, rice vinegar, tahini, sriracha, tamari, and ginger.

3. In a large bowl, combine the peas, cabbage, carrots, bell pepper, green onions, and chickpeas. Coat with half of the dressing mixture and toss well.

4. Add the remaining dressing to the cooled rice and toss to coat. Combine the rice with the vegetables and gently toss. Garnish with pistachios or pumpkin seeds and serve.

Kim's Hint: *You can substitute seasonal vegetables quite easily in this recipe. Chopped avocados make a beautiful garnish for this salad.*

Curly Raw Salad

Incorporating more raw food into one's diet is always a healthy goal, and I have worked to incorporate more raw main entrées into our own meal plan. Summer is the perfect time to increase raw menu options since fresh produce is so abundant. This salad is pretty, delicious, and rich in fiber, vitamins, and minerals. It's also versatile since it's easy to substitute seasonal veggies for many of the ingredients.

Dressing

½ cup orange juice

2 tablespoons low-sodium tamari

2 tablespoons pure maple syrup

1 tablespoon apple cider vinegar

1 tablespoon tahini

1 teaspoon sriracha

1 teaspoon Dijon mustard

1 or 2 garlic cloves, peeled

2 teaspoons grated fresh ginger

Salad

2 cups thinly sliced red cabbage

2 cups chopped kale

2 cups frozen edamame or peas, thawed

2 zucchini, cut into noodles using a julienne peeler or spiralizer

2 carrots, peeled and shredded

1 red or yellow bell pepper, seeded and thinly sliced

4 green onions, thinly sliced

2 tablespoons sesame seeds, for garnish

Yields: 4 to 6 servings
Prep Time: 30 minutes
Cook Time: 0 minutes

1. Combine all the dressing ingredients in a blender and blend until smooth.

2. Combine all the salad ingredients in a large bowl. Toss with the dressing and garnish with the sesame seeds. Serve.

Kim's Hint: *Salad dressings are a subject on which people have strong personal preferences. While some of us love creamy ranch-style dressings, others prefer a lighter vinaigrette. Though I chose an orange dressing for this salad based on my own preference, it can really be paired with any dressing.*

Mayan Salad

This salad is a sweet Mexican-style blend of quinoa, beans, veggies, and avocados. The sweetness comes from the orange juice. The variety of colors, textures, and flavors make this a highly requested salad. It also makes a great filling for a burrito if you have leftovers.

¼ cup orange juice

2 tablespoons red wine vinegar

½ teaspoon ground cumin

Pinch of sea salt

2 mangoes, pitted, peeled, and diced

1 red bell pepper, seeded and diced

1 cup canned or cooked black beans, rinsed and drained

¼ cup chopped fresh cilantro

3 green onions, thinly sliced

1½ cup cooked quinoa

1 avocado, pitted, peeled, and diced, for garnish

¼ cup pumpkin seeds, for garnish

Yields: 4 servings
Prep Time: 20 minutes
Cook Time: 15 minutes

1. In a small bowl, whisk together the orange juice, vinegar, cumin, and sea salt.

2. Combine the mangoes, bell pepper, beans, cilantro, and green onions in a medium bowl and drizzle half of the orange juice mixture over the vegetables. Toss to coat them thoroughly.

3. Add the quinoa to the vegetable mixture, along with the remaining dressing, and toss to combine. Garnish with the avocado and pumpkin seeds and serve.

Kim's Hint: *For a little extra color and flavor, add ½ cup fresh or frozen (thawed) corn.*

Roasted Sweet Potato and Kale Salad

I love a Caesar salad, and this one is delicious. Often the best part of a Caesar salad is the croutons, but roasted sweet potatoes make a fabulous stand-in.

1 medium sweet potato, peeled and diced (¾-inch cubes)

½ teaspoon dried rosemary

¼ teaspoon dried thyme

Sea salt

Black pepper

1 bunch kale

1 small red onion, thinly sliced

¼ to ½ cup Caesar Dressing (page 87)

¼ cup raw sunflower seeds

¼ cup dried cranberries

Yields: 4 servings
Prep Time: 20 minutes
Cook Time: 35 minutes

1. Preheat the oven to 400°F. Line a rimmed baking sheet with parchment paper.

2. Toss the sweet potatoes with the rosemary, thyme, and a pinch each of salt and pepper. Spread out the seasoned sweet potato cubes in a single layer on the prepared baking sheet. Roast the sweet potatoes for about 35 minutes, until they are just barely golden brown on the edges.

3. Strip the kale leaves from their stems. Take a handful of leaves at a time and slice them into thin strips.

4. Combine the kale and onion in a salad bowl. Add 2 tablespoons of the dressing and toss to coat. (You can also massage the dressing into the kale with your fingers for a softer texture.) Add more dressing as needed, depending on the size of the kale bunch you started with and how much dressing you like.

5. Pile the roasted sweet potatoes on top of the dressed kale leaves. Top with the sunflower seeds and cranberries. Serve immediately or refrigerate until ready to eat.

Kim's Hint: *If you are not a kale fan, you can substitute a mix of greens and romaine lettuce.*

Spicy Buffalo Pasta Salad

This lettuce and pasta salad tossed with a creamy Buffalo-style blue cheez dressing is spicy, crunchy, and delicious. This is a fun summertime salad that appeals to both kids and adults. It's also a perfect accompaniment to grilled veggie burgers or veggie kabobs.

Dressing

2 tablespoons raw cashews or almonds

4 ounces extra-firm tofu

3 tablespoons lemon juice

2 to 4 tablespoons Frank's Original Red Hot Sauce

2 tablespoons tahini

1½ tablespoons pure maple syrup

1 teaspoon garlic powder

Salad

8 to 10 ounces whole-grain penne or rotini

2 celery stalks, thinly sliced

2 carrots, peeled and shredded

2 cups peas, fresh or frozen (thawed)

5 cups thinly sliced romaine lettuce (about 2 small hearts)

Yields: 6 servings
Prep Time: 25 minutes
Cook Time: 0 minutes

1. Combine the dressing ingredients in a high-powered blender and blend until smooth and creamy. Set aside.

2. Cook the pasta according to the package instructions. Drain and rinse under cold water.

3. Combine the pasta, celery, carrots, peas, and dressing in a large bowl and toss until thoroughly coated.

4. Just before serving, add the lettuce and toss gently.

Kim's Hint: *If you are making this dish ahead of time, I recommend you always add the lettuce right before serving or it will wilt.*

Sweet Chile Broccoli Salad

This is a unique broccoli salad without the usual mayonnaise base. The dressing is slightly spicy with a little bit of sweetness, which pairs nicely with the broccoli.

Sauce

¼ cup lemon juice

¼ cup water

3 tablespoons low-sodium tamari

3 tablespoons pure maple syrup

1 tablespoon tahini

2 teaspoons sriracha

2 garlic cloves, peeled

Salad

1 head broccoli, cut into small florets

1 red bell pepper, seeded and diced

2 carrots, peeled and shredded

1 cup corn, fresh or frozen (thawed)

½ cup finely chopped red onion

¼ cup sesame seeds

¼ cup chopped walnuts

Yields: 4 servings
Prep Time: 20 minutes
Cook Time: 1 minute

1. Combine the sauce ingredients in a blender and blend until smooth. Set aside.

2. Bring a medium pot of water to a boil over medium-high heat. Add the broccoli florets and blanch for 15 to 20 seconds. Drain in a colander and rinse under cold running water.

3. Transfer the broccoli to a large bowl and add the bell pepper, carrots, corn, red onion, sesame seeds, and walnuts. Add the sauce and toss to combine. Serve.

Sushi Salad

Making sushi can be time consuming, so I created a sushi salad! This hearty rice-and-vegetable dish has many of the unique ingredients you find in sushi, including sweet vinegar and the traditional nori seaweed, without all the fuss.

4½ cups cooked short-grain brown rice

⅓ cup rice vinegar

1 tablespoon pure maple syrup

2 tablespoons low-sodium tamari

3 green onions, sliced

2 medium carrots, shredded

1 cucumber, peeled and diced

1 cup frozen edamame or peas, thawed

2 nori sheets, torn or cut into 1-inch pieces

1 avocado, pitted, peeled, and sliced

2 tablespoons black sesame seeds

Yields: 6 servings
Prep Time: 15 minutes
Cook Time: 0 minutes

Combine all ingredients except avocado and sesame seeds and toss gently. Top with the avocado and garnish with the sesame seeds.

Kim's Hint: *This recipe is simple and fun to modify. Try adding red or yellow peppers, celery, or even water chestnuts for different colors and textures.*

Vibrant Greens and Beet Salad

I love a rich and colorful salad, and this one is a beautiful addition to any meal. The balsamic vinegar brings out the sweetness of the beets and combines with the lime juice and spices for a fresh and fun flavor.

3 tablespoons balsamic vinegar

2 tablespoons lime juice

1 tablespoon Dijon mustard

2 teaspoons pure maple syrup

½ teaspoon garlic powder

¼ teaspoon black pepper

Sea salt to taste

2 to 3 large red beets, cooked and diced

4 cups finely chopped kale

¼ cup slivered almonds, for garnish

Yields: 4 servings
Prep Time: 20
Cook Time: 0 minutes

In a large bowl, whisk together the balsamic vinegar, lime juice, Dijon mustard, maple syrup, garlic powder, pepper, and salt in a small bowl. Add the beets and kale and toss until completely coated. Garnish with the slivered almonds and serve.

Kim's Hints:

- *You can often find precooked beets in the produce section of the grocery store.*
- *I love to add things to this dish to make it a meal. My favorite addition is 2 cups of quinoa and some chickpeas. You can also add shredded carrots, edamame, and/or peas.*

Warm German Potato Salad

German potato salad is a sweet and sour potato dish that my mother often brought to potlucks. The traditional version of the dish is typically garnished with plenty of bacon, but in this version there's no need; it's already chock-full of rich, smoky flavors. I prefer to eat it warm, but it can be served cold as well.

2 pounds red potatoes,
   1-inch diced

⅔ cup white vinegar

⅔ cup water

¼ cup pure maple syrup

1 tablespoon Dijon mustard

1½ tablespoons cornstarch

½ teaspoon smoked paprika

¼ teaspoon celery seed

½ teaspoon sea salt

¼ teaspoon black pepper

1 onion, diced

4 garlic cloves, minced

3 celery stalks, sliced

6 green onions, sliced

Yields: 4 to 6 servings
Prep Time: 20 minutes
Cook Time: 20 minutes

1. Put the diced potatoes in a medium saucepan and cover with water. Bring the water to a boil over medium-high heat. Cook the potatoes for about 10 minutes, until they are tender but firm when pierced with a fork. Do not overcook the potatoes or they will turn to mush. Drain and rinse the potatoes in cold water, then set aside to cool.

2. In a small bowl, whisk together the vinegar, water, maple syrup, Dijon mustard, cornstarch, smoked paprika, celery seed, salt, and pepper.

3. Heat a large frying pan over medium-high heat. Sauté the onion, garlic, and celery in a small amount of water until tender, about 8 minutes. Stir in the vinegar mixture and cook until thickened, about 5 minutes.

4. Stir in the potatoes and green onions and cook until the potatoes are heated through. Serve warm.

Appetizers, Dips, and Spreads

Think Outside the Snack Box

When we're looking for snack food, we often turn to a box or bag. We like our snacks to be quick, easy, and convenient—and for many, that means packaged products.

There are a few healthy snacks that meet these requirements, such as baked tortilla chips and dips or salsas, low-fat whole-grain crackers, and oil-free granola bars. And while some of these items, minimally processed and eaten only from time to time, can certainly be part of a healthy diet, if we shift our "snacking mind-set," we see that it can be inexpensive and easy to incorporate whole foods as snacks.

Fruit is always a great choice, but it's helpful to have a variety of options to curb the temptation to open a box or bag. Instead of your usual processed snack, consider these:

- Baked potatoes: Bake sweet and white potatoes, whole or in wedges, in batches and store in the refrigerator. Serve with some hummus, bean dip, or other spread.

- Roasted chickpeas, seasoned with garlic, onion powder, and nutritional yeast; a Mexican seasoning blend; or other favorite spices.

- Cut veggies, paired with your favorite oil-free dip.

- Edamame, very lightly salted or seasoned and roasted.

- Nut butter and fruit wraps: Spread a tablespoon or two of your favorite nut butter (with no added oils or sugar) on a whole-grain wrap, top with a sliced banana or other fruit, and roll it up. Cut into halves or quarters for smaller snacks.

- Muesli with unsweetened plant-based milk or a cup of unsweetened applesauce.

- Air-popped popcorn, sprayed with vinegar or tamari and spices.

- Frozen fruit.

- Fruit smoothies or shakes: Blend or simply mix your favorite frozen berries and unsweetened plant-based milk.

Mango Salsa

This sweet, citrus-flavored salsa goes great in tacos or on a Mexican salad. We also love to add it to our baked potato bar.

1 mango, pitted, peeled, and finely chopped

¼ cup finely chopped red bell pepper

¼ cup finely chopped red onion

3 green onions, sliced

1 jalapeño pepper, seeded and minced

¼ cup chopped fresh cilantro

2 tablespoons lime juice

1 tablespoon lemon juice

Sea salt to taste

Black pepper to taste

Yields: 8 servings
Prep Time: 15 minutes
Cook Time: 0 minutes

Toss together all the ingredients in a bowl and let stand for 30 minutes before serving.

Buffalo-Style Hummus

I love the vinegar and heat in Buffalo sauce, so I folded it into my hummus! This is definitely a hit in our house. It goes great on a veggie burger or in a wrap loaded with your choice of veggies.

3 garlic cloves, peeled

¼ cup Frank's Original Red Hot Sauce, or more to taste

2 tablespoons tahini

2 tablespoons lemon juice

2 tablespoons white vinegar

2 (15-ounce) cans chickpeas, rinsed and drained, or 3 cups cooked chickpeas

Sea salt to taste

¼ teaspoon paprika, for garnish

Yields: 6 servings
Prep Time: 10 minutes
Cook Time: 0 minutes

Combine the garlic, hot sauce, tahini, lemon juice, and white vinegar in a food processor and blend until mixed well. Add the chickpeas and season with sea salt to taste. Process until smooth. Sprinkle with paprika and serve.

Kim's Hint: *Hummus can take on almost any flavor you desire. The PlantPure Nation Cookbook includes a standard hummus recipe, which can be altered with herbs, spices, and vegetables to create any kind of hummus spread you like.*

Carrot Hummus

This slightly sweet and savory hummus is perfect as a dip or sandwich filler.

4 carrots, peeled and cut into large chunks

3 garlic cloves, peeled

¼ cup water

¼ cup lemon juice

2 tablespoons tahini

1 (15-ounce) can chickpeas, rinsed and drained, or 1½ cups cooked chickpeas

1 teaspoon ground cumin

¼ teaspoon sea salt

¼ teaspoon black pepper

Yields: 4 to 6 servings
Prep Time: 15 minutes
Cook Time: 15 minutes

1. Put the carrots in a medium a pot and add just enough water to cover them. Bring to a boil over high heat, reduce the heat to medium-low, and cook until tender, 10 to 15 minutes. Drain and rinse under cold running water.

2. Combine the garlic, water, lemon juice, and tahini in a food processor and blend until mixed well. Add the cooked carrots, chickpeas, cumin, salt, and pepper and process until smooth. Serve.

Buffalo-Style Hummus

Asparagus Roll-Ups

I love bean dips and asparagus and wanted a healthy alternative to similar recipes that use cream cheese for filling. The result was this easy and beautiful appetizer.

1 (15-ounce) can cannellini beans, rinsed and drained, or 1½ cups cooked cannellini beans

1 tablespoon Dijon mustard

2 teaspoons lemon juice

¼ teaspoon liquid smoke

2 tablespoons nutritional yeast flakes

1 teaspoon garlic powder

1 teaspoon smoked paprika, divided

12 slices 100% whole wheat bread

24 asparagus spears

Yields: 6 to 8 servings
Prep Time: 30 minutes
Cook Time: 10 minutes

1. Preheat the oven to 425°F. Line a rimmed baking sheet with parchment paper.

2. Combine the beans, mustard, lemon juice, liquid smoke, nutritional yeast flakes, garlic powder, and ½ teaspoon of the smoked paprika in a food processor and blend until smooth and creamy. Set aside.

3. Cut off the crusts from the bread and flatten each piece with a rolling pin until very thin.

4. Trim the tough ends of each asparagus spear so they measure 1 to 2 inches longer than the flattened bread.

5. Spread about 2 tablespoons of the bean mixture onto a flattened slice of bread. If this seems too thick to roll, you may need to use less. Place two asparagus spears along the edge of the bread and roll it up. Repeat with the remaining ingredients.

6. Place the rolls, seam side down, on the prepared baking sheet and sprinkle with the remaining ½ teaspoon smoked paprika. Bake for 10 minutes, or until the bread becomes crispy and slightly golden around the edges. Serve warm.

Kim's Hint: *You can choose any type of bread for this recipe as long as it's soft enough to roll out very flat.*

Deviled Mushrooms

A picnic just isn't the same without deviled *something*. These mushrooms are a fun finger food that will have everyone raving.

24 button mushrooms, stems removed

1 (15-ounce) can cannellini beans, rinsed and drained, or 1½ cups cooked cannellini beans

1 tablespoon water

2 teaspoons Dijon mustard

1½ teaspoons apple cider vinegar

1 tablespoon nutritional yeast flakes

½ teaspoon garlic powder

¼ teaspoon ground turmeric

¼ teaspoon sea salt

¼ teaspoon paprika, for garnish

Yields: 6 to 8 servings
Prep Time: 20 minutes
Cook Time: 15 minutes

1. Preheat the oven to 400°F. Line a rimmed baking sheet with parchment paper.

2. Place the mushrooms, destemmed side up, on the prepared baking sheet. Bake for 20 minutes, or until slightly browned. Set aside to cool.

3. In a food processor, combine the beans, water, mustard, vinegar, nutritional yeast flakes, garlic powder, turmeric, and salt. Process until smooth and creamy.

4. To serve, spoon small amounts of the bean filling into each mushroom cap and sprinkle with paprika.

Kim's Hints:

- *You can save time by using raw mushroom caps, but I like to roast them because I prefer a chewier texture.*
- *Instead of using a spoon, you can transfer the bean dip to a zip-top bag, snip off one corner, and pipe it into the mushroom caps.*

Whole-Grain Crackers

I love Mary's Gone Crackers and found a recipe that mimics them pretty well—no dehydrator necessary! However, I wanted to feature the flavors of sour cream and onion (without the dairy, of course!), so I used a few extra seasonings in my version. This is a great recipe for using up leftover rice or quinoa. These crackers are crunchy, flavorful, and gluten free and go great with hummus or your favorite dip.

1 cup cooked brown rice

1 cup cooked quinoa

¼ cup chia seeds

¼ cup flax meal

¼ cup sesame seeds

2 tablespoons nutritional yeast flakes

1½ tablespoons apple cider vinegar

1 tablespoon onion powder

1 teaspoon garlic powder

¼ teaspoon sea salt

2 to 3 tablespoons lemon juice

Kim's Hint: *Instead of using 1 cup each quinoa and brown rice, you can to use 2 cups of a blended grain. My favorite is TruRoots sprouted rice and quinoa blend.*

Yields: 4 to 6 servings
Prep Time: 20 minutes
Cook Time: 30 minutes

1. Preheat the oven to 350°F.

2. Combine all the ingredients except the lemon juice in a food processor and process until it becomes a slightly sticky mixture. Add the lemon juice a tablespoon at a time until you have a sticky dough that forms a ball. It should have the consistency of stiff cookie dough. Divide the dough in half and form two balls.

3. Place one dough ball on a sheet of parchment paper and press down on it slightly. Cover the dough with plastic wrap and roll it out into a very thin, irregularly shaped sheet. You can make your crackers as thin or as thick as you like, but thicker crackers will take longer to cook.

4. Remove the plastic wrap and place the parchment paper and cracker dough on a large baking sheet. Repeat with the remaining dough and place on a second baking sheet.

5. Bake for 15 minutes and remove the pans from the oven to flip the dough. You will notice the edges beginning to brown and curl at this point. Don't worry if the sheet of dough breaks when you flip it since you will be breaking it apart anyway.

6. Bake for another 10 minutes. Remove from the oven and break into irregular cracker-size pieces. Bake for an additional 5 to 8 minutes, until the edges begin to brown. Serve warm or set aside to cool and store in an airtight container for up to a week.

Layered Taco Salad Dip

This plant-based, oil-free appetizer is always a huge crowd pleaser. I use the same layers as a traditional taco dip, except I substitute Tofu-Cashew Mayonnaise for the sour cream. Use a glass dish if you have one to show off the pretty layers.

1 cup Tofu-Cashew Mayonnaise (page 94) or Nut-Free Mayonnaise (page 95)

2 teaspoons Mrs. Dash Mexican seasoning

1 (15-ounce) can vegetarian refried beans (no added oils)

1 cup salsa

1 (4-ounce) can sliced black olives, drained

2 cups shredded lettuce

1 large tomato, chopped

1 cup corn, fresh or frozen (thawed)

2 avocados, pitted, peeled, and diced

½ cup chopped green onions

Baked tortilla chips or pita slices, for serving

Yields: 6 to 8 servings
Prep Time: 45 minutes
Cook Time: 0 minutes

1. In a small bowl, mix the mayonnaise and Mexican seasoning. Cover and chill for 30 minutes.

2. In another small bowl, mix the refried beans and salsa until evenly blended.

3. Spread the beans and salsa in the bottom of an 8-inch square glass baking dish. Spread the mayonnaise mixture over the beans. Layer on the olives, lettuce, tomatoes, corn, avocados, and green onions, in that order. Serve with baked tortilla chips or pita slices.

Homemade Vegan Cheez

I wanted to experiment with making my own plant-based cheese, so I searched the web and YouTube for ideas on how to make an oil-free cheese. I didn't have much luck, but I did learn about agar! Agar is a type of seaweed that comes in a powdered form and becomes gelatinous when dissolved in water and cooked, so it's a great substitute for gelatin. It's expensive, but a little goes a long way. You can find it at most natural food stores. Agar flakes also work, but you will need more, since 1 teaspoon agar powder equals 2 tablespoons agar flakes.

2 cups unsweetened plant-based milk, divided

¾ cup raw cashews

3 tablespoons lemon juice

2 tablespoons tahini

2 tablespoons white miso

1 teaspoon Dijon mustard

¼ cup nutritional yeast flakes

1 teaspoon onion powder

½ teaspoon garlic powder

1 teaspoon sea salt

8 teaspoons agar powder

½ cup chopped pimiento (optional)

1 tablespoon dried chives (optional)

Yields: 6 servings
Prep Time: 30 minutes, plus 3 hours to chill
Cook Time: 10 minutes

1. Line two ramekins, custard cups, or other small ceramic or glass bowls with parchment paper. (This is not necessary but it makes removal of the cheese easier later.)

2. Combine 1 cup of the milk, the cashews, lemon juice, tahini, white miso, Dijon mustard, nutritional yeast, onion powder, garlic powder, and salt in a high-powered blender and blend until smooth and creamy.

3. Combine the remaining 1 cup milk and the agar in a medium saucepan and cook over medium-high heat until the agar is dissolved. Reduce the heat to medium-low. The mixture will begin to thicken.

4. When the milk and agar powder has thickened, pour the creamy mixture from the blender into the hot milk and agar mixture. Stir continuously as the mixture thickens. Stir in the pimiento and chives (if using). Transfer the mixture to the prepared ramekins.

5. Cover the ramekins with plastic wrap and refrigerate until the cheese is firm, 3 to 4 hours. Lift the parchment paper or use a knife to lift the cheese from the ramekin. Grate or slice the cheese to serve.

Kim's Hint: *You can add many flavorings to make this cheese unique. I have added minced jalapeño, 2 cooked carrots (blended with the cashews), vegan bacon bits, a touch of liquid smoke, and even chopped black or green olives.*

Spicy Nacho Sauce

You won't miss a traditional nacho sauce after you try this recipe, especially since it's so easy to make. We like to keep a container of this in the refrigerator so it's always on hand for topping baked potatoes, tacos, pizza, or tortilla chips.

½ cup raw cashews

1½ cups water

2 teaspoons lemon juice

2 garlic cloves, peeled

2 tablespoons nutritional yeast flakes

1½ teaspoons cornstarch

1 teaspoon smoked paprika

1 teaspoon onion powder

½ teaspoon sea salt

½ teaspoon ground cumin

¼ teaspoon chipotle chile powder, or more to taste

1 jalapeño, seeded and minced

1 (4-ounce) can diced green chiles, drained

Yields: 4 servings
Prep Time: 10 minutes
Cook Time: 5 minutes

1. Combine all the ingredients, except the jalapeño and diced green chiles, in a high-powered blender and blend on high until creamy and smooth. Add the jalapeño and diced green chiles.

2. Transfer the mixture to a saucepan and cook over medium-high heat until bubbly and thickened, about 5 minutes. Serve. Store leftovers in the refrigerator for up to 5 days.

Kim's Hint: *If you want to reduce the quantity of cashews, use ¼ cup and add 1 tablespoon cornstarch to the blender. For a completely nut-free version, replace the cashews with 2 cups mashed sweet potatoes, use an unsweetened plant-based milk instead of the water, and add 2 tablespoons cornstarch. You may find that this version does not pack the punch of the original.*

Slow Cooker Apple Butter

Growing up in upstate New York meant I was surrounded by apples every fall. I had the added benefit of living near Cornell University, where they have some amazing orchards and the best apples and cider ever! This apple butter is perfect for spreading on breakfast toast or adding to a bowl of oatmeal as a sweetener instead of maple syrup.

3 pounds apples (about 12 apples)

2 tablespoons apple cider vinegar

½ cup Sucanat

2 tablespoons ground cinnamon

1 teaspoon ground allspice

¼ teaspoon ground cloves

2 teaspoons pure vanilla extract

Yields: 3 to 4 cups
Prep Time: 15 minutes
Cook Time: 10 to 13 hours

1. Wash, core, and quarter the apples. There is no need to peel the apples since the peel contains lots of fiber and nutrients that will be pureed later in the process. Combine the apples, vinegar, Sucanat, cinnamon, allspice, and cloves in a slow cooker. Cover and cook on low for 8 to 10 hours. Stir and continue cooking for another 2 to 3 hours. Stir in the vanilla.

2. Let the apple mixture cool completely, then transfer to a food processor or blender. (Alternatively, you can use an immersion blender for this step.) Blend until there are no chunks remaining. You may need to do this in batches.

3. Pour into jars and store in the refrigerator for up to 2 weeks. You can also freeze it for 3 to 4 months.

Kim's Hints:

- You can use any variety or combination of varieties of apple you like, but sweeter apples are especially nice for this recipe.
- I often put this recipe in the slow cooker in the evening before bed. By morning, it is almost completely finished. What a wonderful smell to wake up to!

Walnut Pesto

This pesto works great tossed in a pasta, as a sauce for pizza, or even as a sandwich spread. The walnuts and nutritional yeast give it that perfect creamy, cheesy flavor. We've found that a blend of basil and spinach is an inexpensive alternative during the off-season, but you can certainly use all basil.

2 cups packed fresh basil

2 cups packed spinach

1 cup walnuts

3 garlic cloves, peeled

2 tablespoons water

2 tablespoons lemon juice

3 tablespoons nutritional yeast flakes

¼ teaspoon sea salt

¼ teaspoon black pepper

Yields: 4 servings
Prep Time: 15 minutes
Cook Time: 0 minutes

1. Combine the basil, spinach, walnuts, and garlic in a food processor. Pulse until the mixture is coarsely ground.

2. Add the water, lemon juice, nutritional yeast flakes, salt, and pepper and continue pulsing until you have a thick paste. Serve.

Kim's Hints:

- *To make this nut-free, replace the walnuts with cooked or canned white beans or chickpeas, or fresh green peas. The consistency will be smoother, but the flavor is still amazing!*
- *I like to freeze pesto in ice cube trays; simply spoon 1 tablespoon pesto into each freezer tray cube. Once frozen, transfer the pesto cubes to a zip-top bag and freeze for later use.*

Soups and Stews

Instant Pot

I don't have a relationship with the company that makes the Instant Pot, but I must confess: I love this cookware. It is a powerhouse when it comes to cooking at different pressures and speeds. This one machine does the work of seven: It's a rice cooker, slow cooker, pressure cooker, sauté pan, yogurt maker, steamer, and warmer.

I use mine mainly for pressure cooking and slow cooking. When I first got my Instant Pot, I started cooking all our dried beans and grains in it. I then froze what I cooked, and soon I had a variety of freezer bags loaded with items that usually take hours to cook!

Although I do not include Instant Pot directions in this cookbook, feel free to give it a try for most of my recipes, especially those that include lentils, rice, or grains. You can cook them in a fraction of the time and in a way that truly locks in the flavors. You also retain more of the nutrients of the food you are cooking,

Photo Courtesy of Instant Pot

since you are using less water and cooking for a shorter amount of time.

The price of these cooking pots is around $100, depending on the size and where you order. If you go to PlantPureNation.com, we offer a coupon code that will allow you to receive a bigger discount than is offered through many other organizations. It is definitely my most-used kitchen appliance, and I think you will find that it makes going plant-based much easier.

Pumpkin Soup

This is an easy soup that is perfect for the fall season. It's also great with or over a baked potato or pasta for a complete meal.

1 medium leek, chopped

1 cup chopped apple

1 (16-ounce) can 100% pumpkin puree (not pumpkin pie filling)

3½ cups unsweetened plant-based milk

3 garlic cloves, minced

½ teaspoon ground cinnamon

½ teaspoon ground ginger

¼ teaspoon ground nutmeg

½ teaspoon sea salt

¼ teaspoon black pepper

Yields: 4 servings
Prep Time: 15 minutes
Cook Time: 15 minutes

1. In a large stockpot over medium-high heat, sauté the leek and apple in a small amount of water until tender, about 8 minutes.

2. Reduce the heat to medium and add the pumpkin, milk, garlic, cinnamon, ginger, nutmeg, salt, and pepper. Cook for another 10 to 15 minutes.

3. Puree the mixture in a blender or use an immersion blender to obtain a creamy consistency. Serve warm.

Cream of Broccoli Soup

This is an easy soup to prepare, and kids love the creamy texture. We often use this soup as a topping for our baked potato dinners.

1 onion, diced

2 celery stalks, diced

1 large russet potato, peeled and diced

1 (16-ounce) bag frozen broccoli florets or 5 cups chopped fresh broccoli florets

2 cups low-sodium vegetable broth

3 cups unsweetened plant-based milk

¼ cup whole wheat flour

3 tablespoons nutritional yeast flakes

1 teaspoon garlic powder

⅛ teaspoon ground nutmeg

½ teaspoon sea salt

¼ teaspoon black pepper

Yields: 4 to 6 servings
Prep Time: 20 minutes
Cook Time: 30 minutes

1. In a large stockpot over medium-high heat, sauté the onion and celery in a small amount of water until tender, about 8 minutes. Add the potato, broccoli, and vegetable broth. Continue cooking for 15 minutes, or until the potatoes are tender.

2. Transfer the vegetable mixture to a blender and blend until you achieve the texture you prefer—chunky or smooth. Return the vegetable mixture to the pot. Do not bother rinsing out the blender.

3. Combine the milk, whole wheat flour, nutritional yeast flakes, garlic powder, nutmeg, salt, and pepper in the blender. Blend until the mixture is smooth and the flour is completely absorbed.

4. Add the milk mixture to the pureed vegetables in the pot. Simmer on low for 15 minutes, until bubbly and thickened. Serve warm.

Creamy White Bean Soup

This delicious, creamy soup will remind you of traditional white bean soup, but without the ham. It's easy to make, comforting, and full of flavor.

1 onion, diced

2 celery stalks, diced

2 carrots, peeled and diced

4 garlic cloves, minced

1 cup low-sodium vegetable broth

1 cup water

3 (15-ounce) cans cannellini beans, rinsed and drained, or 4½ cups cooked cannellini beans, divided

1 teaspoon smoked paprika

½ teaspoon dried rosemary

¼ teaspoon dried thyme

½ teaspoon sea salt

¼ teaspoon black pepper

¼ cup chopped fresh parsley

Yields: 4 to 6 servings
Prep Time: 20 minutes
Cook Time: 30 minutes

1. In a large stockpot over medium-high heat, sauté the onion, celery, carrots, and garlic in a small amount of water until tender, about 8 minutes.

2. Combine the vegetable broth, water, and 2 cans of cannellini beans in a blender. Blend until smooth and creamy.

3. Add the blended beans to the vegetables in the pot, along with the remaining 1 can of whole beans and all the seasonings. Simmer on low for 20 to 30 minutes to allow the flavors to bloom. Serve warm.

Easy Black Bean Soup

This hearty soup takes just a few minutes to prepare. I love serving it with a baked potato or over a whole grain such as rice or quinoa.

1 onion, diced

1 green bell pepper, seeded and diced

1 jalapeño pepper, seeded and minced

5 garlic cloves, minced

2 (15-ounce) cans black beans, rinsed and drained, or 3 cups cooked black beans

1 cup low-sodium vegetable broth

2 cups salsa

1 tablespoon chili powder

1 teaspoon ground cumin

Sea salt to taste

1 cup corn, fresh or frozen

¼ cup chopped fresh cilantro, for garnish

Yields: 4 servings
Prep Time: 10 minutes
Cook Time: 20 minutes

1: In a large stockpot over medium-high heat, sauté the onion, bell pepper, jalapeño, and garlic in a small amount of water until tender, about 8 minutes.

2. Reduce the heat to medium and add the black beans, vegetable broth, salsa, chili powder, cumin, and salt to taste. Cook for 10 to 15 minutes. While the soup is cooking, scoop out half of the soup and process in a blender until smooth and creamy. Return the pureed mixture to the pot. (Alternatively, you can use an immersion blender to partially puree the soup right in the pot.)

3. Stir in the corn and continue cooking for another 5 to 10 minutes. Serve warm, garnished with the cilantro.

Kim's Hint:
I like Muir Glen salsa because it is low sodium and has a great fresh flavor.

Green Curry Coconut Soup

Everyone loves vegetable soup, and Thai green curry paste gives this one a tantalizing, mild curry flavor. You can also serve this soup over a grain for a heartier meal.

2 red onions, halved then thinly sliced

2 large carrots, peeled and diced

8 ounces button mushrooms, sliced

4 garlic cloves, minced

1 tablespoon grated fresh ginger

1 (15-ounce) can lite coconut milk

2 tablespoons green curry paste

3 tablespoons whole wheat flour

2 cups roughly chopped spinach

1 cup chopped fresh basil

1 (15-ounce) can chickpeas, rinsed and drained, or 1½ cups cooked chickpeas

2 cups low-sodium vegetable broth

1 tablespoon lime juice

Sea salt to taste

Yields: 4 to 6 servings
Prep Time: 20 minutes
Cook Time: 30 minutes

1. In a large stockpot over medium-high heat, sauté the onions, carrots, mushrooms, garlic, and ginger in a small amount of water until tender, about 8 minutes.

2. In a small bowl, whisk together the coconut milk, green curry paste, and flour until creamy.

3. Add the coconut milk mixture to the pot, along with the remaining ingredients. Reduce the heat to low and simmer for 20 to 30 minutes. Serve warm.

Kim's Hint: *I sometimes puree the fresh basil with the coconut milk, curry paste, and flour in a blender. This will turn your soup green but result in a deeper basil flavor.*

Mushroom Corn Chowder

This is a delicious and hearty chowder loaded with the perfect blend of veggies. The mushrooms in this recipe really create a chewy, meaty texture while the beans and cashews make the creamy base. It's truly a comfort meal in a bowl!

1 (15-ounce) can cannellini beans, rinsed and drained, or 1½ cups cooked cannellini beans

4 cups low-sodium vegetable broth

¼ cup raw cashews

3 tablespoons whole wheat flour

2 onions, halved then thinly sliced

4 garlic cloves, minced

8 ounces shiitake mushrooms, sliced

8 ounces button mushrooms, sliced

1 pound red potatoes, diced (3 or 4 medium potatoes)

8 to 10 ounces spinach, torn into bite-size pieces, or baby spinach

2 cups corn, fresh or frozen (thawed)

1 teaspoon dried dill

½ teaspoon dried thyme

½ teaspoon sea salt

½ teaspoon black pepper

3 tablespoons chopped fresh parsley, for garnish

Yields: 6 servings
Prep Time: 20 minutes
Cook Time: 40 minutes

1. In a high-powered blender, blend the cannellini beans, vegetable broth, cashews, and flour on high for 1 to 2 minutes until smooth and creamy. Set aside.

2. In a large stockpot over medium-high heat, sauté the onions, garlic, and mushrooms in a small amount of water until tender, about 8 minutes.

3. Add the creamy bean mixture, potatoes, spinach, corn, dill, and thyme. Reduce the heat to medium-low and cook for 20 to 30 minutes, until the potatoes are tender. Season with the salt and pepper and serve warm, garnished with the fresh parsley.

Classic Red Chili

A big pot of traditional chili is always a popular dish. This recipe is loaded with veggies and beans and a medley of sweet, spicy, and savory flavors. It also makes a wonderful slow cooker recipe, since the longer you cook any tomato-based sauce, the richer the flavor.

1 onion, diced

2 celery stalks, sliced

1 red or green bell pepper, seeded and diced

1 poblano pepper, seeded and minced

4 garlic cloves, minced

1 (15-ounce) can black beans, rinsed and drained, or 1½ cups cooked black beans

1 (15-ounce) can red kidney beans, rinsed and drained, or 1½ cups cooked red kidney beans

1 (28-ounce) can crushed tomatoes

½ cup tomato paste

¼ cup bulgur wheat

1 cup corn, fresh or frozen

1 tablespoon molasses

1 tablespoon apple cider vinegar

1 tablespoon chili powder

1 teaspoon ground cumin

1 teaspoon dried oregano

½ teaspoon sea salt

¼ teaspoon black pepper

½ cup sliced green onions, for garnish

½ cup chopped fresh cilantro, for garnish

Yields: 6 servings
Prep Time: 20 minutes
Cook Time: 30 minutes

1. In a large stockpot over medium-high heat, sauté the onion, celery, bell pepper, poblano, and garlic in a small amount of water until the onion becomes translucent, about 8 minutes.

2. Reduce the heat to medium and add the remaining ingredients (except the garnish). Cook for 20 to 30 minutes, stirring occasionally. Add more water if you prefer a thinner consistency.

3. Garnish with the green onions and cilantro and serve warm.

Kim's Hint: *This recipe is a fabulous dinner when served over pasta and drizzled with our Spicy Nacho Sauce (page 140). Kids of all ages love a good chili mac!*

Lentil Stew

This traditional lentil stew is easy to prepare and full of rich flavors thanks to the combination of molasses, mustard, and spices. It's a simple one-pot delight.

1 small onion, finely diced

2 large carrots, peeled and finely diced

2 large celery stalks, finely diced

2 russet potatoes, peeled and diced

1 (15-ounce) can diced tomatoes, undrained

1 cup green lentils, rinsed and drained

6 cups water

2 tablespoons molasses

1 tablespoon vegan Worcestershire sauce

1 tablespoon Dijon mustard

1 bay leaf

1 teaspoon dried thyme

6 ounces spinach, torn into bite-size pieces, or baby spinach

½ teaspoon sea salt

Yields: 4 to 6 servings
Prep Time: 20 minutes
Cook Time: 40 minutes

1. In a large stockpot, combine all the ingredients except the spinach and salt. Bring the liquid to a boil over medium-high heat. Reduce the heat to medium-low and simmer until the lentils are softened, 30 to 40 minutes. (Alternatively, you can cook the soup in a slow cooker, covered, for 3 to 4 hours on high.)

2. Just before serving, gently fold in the spinach and stir until wilted, 2 to 3 minutes. Season the stew with the salt and serve.

Moroccan Stew

This stew has a unique flavor thanks to the blend of Moroccan-style spices. I love serving this dish with a grain or bread on a cold evening.

1 red onion, sliced

6 to 8 garlic cloves, minced

1 medium eggplant, cut into ½-inch cubes

2½ cups water, divided

3 tablespoons low-sodium tamari

2 carrots, peeled and thinly sliced

1 red bell pepper, seeded and chopped

1 sweet potato, peeled and diced

2 cups chopped spinach

1 (28-ounce) can diced tomatoes, undrained

1 (15-ounce) can chickpeas, rinsed and drained, or 1½ cups cooked chickpeas

½ cup finely chopped pitted dates

1 tablespoon smoked paprika

1 teaspoon ground cumin

1 teaspoon ground cinnamon

¾ teaspoon ground ginger

½ teaspoon black pepper

¼ teaspoon red pepper flakes

⅛ teaspoon ground cloves

Yields: 4 to 6 servings
Prep Time: 20 minutes
Cook Time: 30 minutes

1. In a large stockpot over medium-high heat, sauté the onion, garlic, eggplant, ½ cup of the water, and tamari until the vegetables are tender, 5 to 10 minutes. Reduce the heat to medium and simmer for another 5 to 10 minutes.

2. Add the carrots and bell pepper and simmer until the carrots are tender, about 8 minutes.

3. Add the remaining 2 cups water and the rest of the ingredients and simmer for another 20 minutes. Serve warm.

Kim's Hint: *Feel free to vary the vegetables in this recipe (except for the eggplant, which is the base of this stew)—try zucchini, parsnips, celery, peas, green beans, corn, white potatoes, or butternut squash. For a spicier version, I like to add minced jalapeños.*

Vegetable Chickpea Stew

This stew has a mild flavor but is hearty enough to serve as a main course if you pair it with your favorite grain.

1 onion, diced

4 garlic cloves, minced

2 medium russet potatoes, peeled and diced

1 medium head cauliflower, cut into bite-size pieces

1 (28-ounce) can diced tomatoes, undrained

2 (15-ounce) cans chickpeas, rinsed and drained, or 3 cups cooked chickpeas

2 cups peas, fresh or frozen

2 teaspoons grated fresh ginger

2 cups water

1 tablespoon pure maple syrup

1 tablespoon curry powder

½ teaspoon black pepper

⅛ teaspoon red pepper flakes

10 ounces spinach, torn into bite-size pieces, or baby spinach

1 teaspoon sea salt

Yields: 6 servings
Prep Time: 20 minutes
Cook Time: 30 minutes

1. In a large stockpot over medium-high heat, sauté the onion and garlic in a small amount of water until tender, about 8 minutes.

2. Add the remaining ingredients, except the spinach and salt, and bring the liquid to a boil. Reduce the heat to medium-low and simmer for 20 to 30 minutes.

3. Transfer about one-third of the soup to a blender and blend until smooth and creamy. Return the pureed mixture to the soup pot. (Alternatively, you can use an immersion blender to partially puree the soup right in the pot.)

4. Just before serving, add the spinach and stir until wilted, 2 to 3 minutes. Season with the salt and serve.

Entrées

Mindful Eating and Cooking

One of the top complaints about adopting a plant-based lifestyle is the amount of time involved. Planning menus, grocery shopping, cooking, cleaning up, and packing lunches are often seen as chores to be squeezed into an already busy schedule. Shifting our thinking about this time, however, and cultivating a greater appreciation for food may actually make these daily tasks enjoyable. Rather than rushing, carve out sufficient time for visiting the farmers' market or grocery store and for cooking; think of it as a break from your work and daily routine.

Often we find it difficult to enjoy something if we feel we should be doing something else that is seen as "more important." Think of the time spent on preparing and eating healthful foods as time gained, rather than time lost. Investing in the health and well-being of your family is an act of mindfulness, so give yourself permission to enjoy the process.

Pasta with White Bean Basil Sauce

This creamy sauce is bursting with flavor—perfect to make when basil is in season. Here I serve it tossed with pasta, but it also goes nicely over a baked potato.

8 ounces whole-grain pasta

1 (15-ounce) can cannellini beans, rinsed and drained, or 1½ cups cooked Great Northern beans

¼ cup water, or more if needed

2 tablespoons lemon juice

1 tablespoon tahini

1 tablespoon Dijon mustard

2 or 3 Medjool dates, pitted

4 garlic cloves, peeled

2 cups fresh basil leaves

2 tablespoons nutritional yeast flakes

¼ teaspoon sea salt

Yields: 2 servings
Prep Time: 10 minutes
Cook Time: 15 minutes

1. Cook the pasta according to the package instructions. Drain and set aside.

2. Combine the remaining ingredients in a blender and blend until creamy and smooth. Transfer the sauce to a saucepan and warm over medium heat. Toss the sauce with the pasta and serve.

Asian Stewed Tofu

This dish was created by our very own PlantPure Nation staff member Jason Boyer. Jason is the director of our online store and also a very talented cook. His recipe has the uniquely warm flavors commonly found in Asian cuisine. He recommends serving this dish over brown rice or soba noodles.

7 ounces extra-firm tofu, cut into ½-inch cubes

1 medium onion, diced

2 celery stalks, diced

2 carrots, peeled and diced

1 (15-ounce) can black beans, rinsed and drained, or 1½ cups cooked black beans

½ teaspoon garlic powder

¼ teaspoon Chinese five-spice powder

¼ teaspoon ground ginger

¼ teaspoon black pepper

¼ teaspoon red pepper flakes

1¼ cups water

2 tablespoons Hoisin Sauce (page 97)

1 tablespoon low-sodium tamari

1 tablespoon tomato paste

1 tablespoon cornstarch

Yields: 4 servings
Prep Time: 20 minutes
Cook Time: 35 minutes

1. Preheat the oven to 375°F. Line a rimmed baking sheet with parchment paper.

2. Place the tofu cubes in a single layer on the prepared baking sheet and bake for 20 to 30 minutes, until the tofu is slightly golden around the edges. Set aside.

3. Meanwhile, in a large skillet over medium-high heat, sauté the onion, celery, and carrots in a small amount of water until the onion is translucent, about 8 minutes. Add the black beans, garlic powder, Chinese five-spice powder, ginger, black pepper, and red pepper flakes.

4. In a small bowl, whisk together the water, hoisin, tamari, tomato paste, and cornstarch until completely blended. Add this mixture to the skillet, reduce the heat to medium-low, and cook for 15 minutes. Add the baked tofu and simmer for an additional 5 to 10 minutes. Serve warm.

Kim's Hint: *Chinese five-spice powder is what gives this dish its unique flavor. You can always add more if you enjoy its star anise, clove, and cinnamon flavors, but I recommend adding it only in pinches since a little can go a long way.*

Aztec Quinoa

This one-pot meal makes dinner preparation quick and easy. While it's great on its own, it also makes a wonderful filling for a taco dinner or a salad-style burrito bowl served with greens, salsa, and lots of avocado slices or guacamole.

1 red bell pepper, seeded and diced

1 red onion, diced

4 garlic cloves, minced

1 small jalapeño or poblano pepper, seeded and minced

1 cup quinoa

1 cup low-sodium vegetable broth

1 (15-ounce) can diced tomatoes, undrained

1 (15-ounce) can black beans, rinsed and drained, or 1½ cups cooked black beans

1 cup frozen corn

¼ cup lime juice

1 teaspoon chili powder

½ teaspoon ground cumin

Sea salt to taste

Black pepper to taste

1 avocado, pitted, peeled, and diced, for serving

¼ cup chopped fresh cilantro, for serving

Yields: 4 servings
Prep Time: 10 minutes
Cook Time: 20 minutes

Combine all the ingredients in a large stockpot, except the avocado and cilantro, and bring to a boil over medium-high heat. Reduce the heat to medium-low and simmer until the quinoa is cooked through, 15 to 20 minutes. Top with the avocado and cilantro and serve.

Kim's Hints:

- Poblano peppers are milder than jalapeños, so they will tame the heat a bit.
- You can substitute ¾ cup uncooked instant brown rice, cooked in 1½ cups low-sodium vegetable broth, for the quinoa.

Bourbon Mushrooms

Bourbon mushrooms are traditionally prepared with butter, cream, and beef broth and served with a side of steak. In this recipe, it's the mushrooms that absorb the unique flavors of the savory sauce, while also adding a chewy texture. These mushrooms are especially delicious served over brown rice, mashed or baked potatoes, barley, or whole-grain pasta.

Vegetables

1 pound button or other mushrooms or a combination, sliced

1 onion, halved then thinly sliced

6 garlic cloves, minced

¼ to ½ cup low-sodium vegetable broth

Sauce

½ cup low-sodium vegetable broth, or more as needed

½ cup unsweetened applesauce

¼ cup tomato paste

3 tablespoons balsamic vinegar

2 tablespoons low-sodium tamari

2 tablespoons bourbon, dry white wine, or pineapple juice

1 tablespoon pure maple syrup

1½ tablespoons cornstarch

1 teaspoon grated fresh ginger

⅛ teaspoon red pepper flakes

Yields: 4 servings
Prep Time: 15 minutes
Cook Time: 20 minutes

1. In a large skillet over medium-high heat, sauté the mushrooms, onion, and garlic in a little of the vegetable broth until the mushrooms are tender, about 8 minutes. Add more vegetable broth as needed to keep the vegetables from sticking.

2. In a small bowl, whisk together the sauce ingredients until well combined. Add the sauce to the skillet, reduce the heat to medium, and cook until bubbly and thickened, 3 to 4 minutes. Reduce the heat to low and continue cooking for another 10 minutes. If you like your sauce thinner, add more vegetable broth, ¼ cup at a time. Serve warm over rice, potatoes, barley, or pasta.

Kim's Hint: *I like to use a mix of sliced portobello and shiitake mushrooms for an especially meaty texture. This makes a wonderful addition to a baked potato bar!*

Carrot Loaf

I originally found this dish in the first Moosewood cookbook. However, that recipe called for cheese, butter, and lots of eggs. My family loved the original version many years ago, so I decided to recreate it to be plant-based and oil-free. This is a perfect dinner for the holidays or cold weather. It gets better the longer it sits and so is a perfect leftover lunch as well.

Glaze

¼ cup water

2 tablespoons tomato paste

2 tablespoons pure maple syrup

1 tablespoon balsamic vinegar

1 tablespoon Dijon mustard

Loaf

3 tablespoons flax meal or chia seeds

½ cup water

1 onion, diced

4 garlic cloves, minced

8 ounces mushrooms, sliced

¼ cup dry white wine or additional water

5 cups grated carrots (about 10 medium carrots)

1 cup whole wheat bread crumbs

¾ cup finely ground walnuts

2 tablespoons nutritional yeast flakes

1 teaspoon dried rosemary

1 teaspoon dried thyme

½ teaspoon sea salt

¼ teaspoon black pepper

Yields: 4 to 6 servings
Prep Time: 30 minutes
Cook Time: 35 minutes

1. Preheat the oven to 375°F. Line an 8-inch square baking pan with parchment paper.

2. In a small bowl, whisk together the glaze ingredients. Set aside.

3. In another small bowl, mix the flax meal and water. Set aside to thicken.

4. In a nonstick skillet over medium-high heat, sauté the onion, garlic, and mushrooms in ¼ cup of white wine until tender, about 8 minutes.

5. In a large mixing bowl, combine the carrots, bread crumbs, walnuts, nutritional yeast, rosemary, thyme, salt, and pepper. Add the thickened flax mixture and sautéed vegetables, and mix well so that everything is equally dispersed.

6. Press the carrot mixture into the prepared pan. Spread the glaze evenly over the top of the carrot loaf. Bake for 35 minutes. Let stand for 20 minutes before slicing and serving.

Kim's Hints:

- *I have substituted almonds for walnuts in the past and it still works beautifully. If someone in your household has a nut allergy, you can use 1 cup smashed chickpeas.*
- *For a gluten-free option, replace the bread crumbs with 1 cup cooked brown rice or oatmeal.*

Creole Red Beans and Rice

This is a recipe that we use in our PlantPure frozen entrée line. It's easy to prepare and quite popular with everyone who enjoys Creole flavors. I recommend making a vegan sour cream to top this dish; you can find a recipe on our website and in *The PlantPure Nation Cookbook*.

Salsa

2 tomatoes, diced

1 cucumber, diced

3 green onions, sliced

¼ cup finely chopped fresh cilantro

¼ cup apple cider vinegar

2 teaspoons lime juice

1 teaspoon sriracha

¼ teaspoon sea salt

Creole Beans

2 cups Butler Soy Curls (optional)

4 cups warm water (optional; for rehydrating the Soy Curls)

2 onions, finely diced

6 garlic cloves, minced

4 celery stalks, finely diced

4 carrots, peeled and finely diced

2 green bell peppers, seeded and finely diced

¼ cup dry red wine or additional water

2 (15-ounce) cans red kidney beans, rinsed and drained, or 3 cups cooked red kidney beans

¼ cup tomato paste

2 teaspoons pure maple syrup

2 teaspoons Dijon mustard

1 teaspoon apple cider vinegar

½ teaspoon black pepper

½ teaspoon dried oregano

⅛ teaspoon ground allspice

1 teaspoon sea salt

6 cups cooked brown rice, for serving

Yields: 6 servings
Prep Time: 25 minutes, plus 3 hours to marinate
Cook Time: 1 hour

1. For the salsa, blend all the ingredients and set aside in the refrigerator to marinate for a few hours before serving.

2. If using the Soy Curls, combine them with the water in a medium bowl. Let sit for 10 minutes, or until fully rehydrated, then drain.

3. In a nonstick skillet over medium-high heat, sauté the onions, garlic, celery, carrots, and bell peppers in the red wine until tender, about 8 minutes.

4. Add the drained Soy Curls (if using), beans, tomato paste, maple syrup, mustard, vinegar, black pepper, oregano, and allspice. Reduce the heat to medium and cook for 45 to 60 minutes, until the vegetables are tender. Season with the sea salt and serve over the brown rice. Top with the salsa.

Fishless Fillets

Both kids and adults love finger foods, and this recipe really captures the flavor, texture, and appearance of those traditional fish sticks from the freezer. You can make these fillets into patties or sticks depending on your personal preference. Serve them with your favorite plant-based dressing or mayonnaise—we love them with Creamy Horseradish Sauce (page 96).

2 tablespoons flax meal or chia seeds

5 tablespoons water

1 (15-ounce) can chickpeas, rinsed and drained, or 1½ cups cooked chickpeas

1 (15-ounce) can artichoke hearts, rinsed and drained

½ cup oatmeal

½ cup cooked brown rice

1 nori sheet, torn into small pieces

1 tablespoon lemon juice

1 tablespoon Old Bay Seasoning

½ teaspoon ground mustard

½ teaspoon dried dill

Sea salt

Black pepper

1 cup panko bread crumbs, for coating

Yields: 4 servings
Prep Time: 20 minutes
Cook Time: 25 minutes

1. Preheat the oven to 400°F. Line a baking sheet with parchment paper.

2. In a small bowl, mix the flax meal and water. Set aside to thicken.

3. Pulse the chickpeas in a food processor until finely ground. Add the artichoke hearts near the end of the processing and pulse until coarsely chopped.

4. Transfer the chickpea and artichoke mixture to a large mixing bowl. Add the oatmeal, rice, nori, flax mixture, lemon juice, Old Bay, mustard, dill, salt, and black pepper to taste.

5. Form the dough into four equal patties or into sticks about 1 inch by 3 inches. Coat each patty or stick evenly with the panko crumbs and place them on the prepared baking sheet. Bake for 15 to 25 minutes, until golden. Serve warm.

Kim's Hint: *Instant oatmeal will yield a creamier texture for these fishless fillets.*

Indian Red Lentil Dahl

Red lentils, sweet potatoes, and a touch of curry make this creamy, hearty stew a meal.

2½ cups red lentils

5 cups water

1 sweet potato, peeled and diced

1 celery stalk, diced

1 medium zucchini, diced

1 red onion, diced

6 garlic cloves, minced

1 tablespoon grated fresh ginger

1 (15-ounce) can diced tomatoes, undrained

1 cup canned lite coconut milk

2 tablespoons red curry paste

2 teaspoons curry powder

1 teaspoon chili powder

½ teaspoon ground turmeric

¼ teaspoon cayenne pepper

½ teaspoon sea salt

¼ cup chopped fresh cilantro

Yields: 6 servings
Prep Time: 10 minutes
Cook Time: 40 minutes

1. Combine the lentils and water in a large stockpot and bring to a boil over medium-high heat. Reduce the heat to medium and cook for 10 minutes, stirring every few minutes to prevent burning on the bottom.

2. Add all the remaining ingredients except the salt and cilantro and stir until completely incorporated. Reduce the heat to medium-low and simmer for 25 to 30 minutes. Season with the salt, garnish with the cilantro, and serve warm.

Kim's Hint: *I like Thai Kitchen brand of red curry paste.*

Japanese Curried Vegetables

This recipe, like Asian Stewed Tofu (page 169), was created by PlantPure employee Jason Boyer. Jason has been with PlantPure since long before the film *PlantPure Nation* was created, helping build and tweak recipes from the start. He is fabulous with Asian flavors and vegetables, and this one is truly special, especially served over brown rice or another grain. You can also find this dish in our frozen line. Thank you, Jason!

Curry Sauce

2½ cups unsweetened plant-based milk

½ cup canned lite coconut milk

2 tablespoons tomato paste

1 tablespoon pure maple syrup

¼ cup whole wheat flour

1 tablespoon curry powder

½ teaspoon sea salt

Vegetables

1 medium potato, peeled and diced

1 cup frozen corn

1 cup frozen peas

3 carrots, peeled and julienned

1 onion, thinly sliced

½ red bell pepper, sliced

2 celery stalks, thinly sliced

2 baby bok choy, thinly sliced

Yields: 4 servings
Prep Time: 20 minutes
Cook Time: 15 minutes

1. In a medium bowl, whisk together the sauce ingredients and set aside.

2. In a large saucepan over medium-high heat, sauté the vegetables in a small amount of water until tender, about 8 minutes.

3. Add the curry sauce, reduce the heat to medium, and continue cooking until bubbly and thickened, about 5 minutes. Serve warm.

Malai Kofta (Veggie Balls and Curry Sauce)

Indian restaurants always offer malai kofta on the menu, but it is usually loaded with oil and heavy cream. This version is rich with the flavors and creaminess of the traditional restaurant-style dish but without the oils and dairy. Serve the kofta over brown rice to soak up all the sauce.

Kofta (veggie balls)

1 cup mashed cooked sweet potatoes, fresh or frozen (thawed)

1 tablespoon flax meal or chia seeds

3 tablespoons water

1 (15-ounce) can chickpeas, rinsed and drained, or 1½ cups cooked chickpeas

½ cup finely ground walnuts

1 cup peas, fresh or frozen (thawed)

1½ cups whole wheat bread crumbs

1 tablespoon grated fresh ginger

1 teaspoon garlic powder

½ teaspoon garam masala

1 teaspoon ground cumin

½ teaspoon black pepper

¼ teaspoon sea salt

Malai (creamy curry sauce)

½ cup raw cashews

2 cups water

¼ cup canned lite coconut milk

2 teaspoons cornstarch

1 tablespoon curry powder

1 teaspoon garam masala

1 teaspoon ground cumin

¼ teaspoon red pepper flakes

3 tablespoons tomato paste

2 teaspoons pure maple syrup

1 onion, diced

6 garlic cloves, minced

1 tablespoon grated fresh ginger

1 teaspoon toasted fennel seeds

½ to 1 teaspoon sea salt

1½ cups frozen peas

Yields 4 to 6 servings
Prep Time: 25 minutes
Cook Time: 30 to 40 minutes

1. Preheat the oven to 400°F. Line a rimmed baking sheet with parchment paper.

2. Boil and mash the sweet potato.

3. Combine the flax meal and water in a small bowl and set aside to thicken.

4. In a food processor, pulse the chickpeas until chopped and slightly smashed but not pureed.

5. Transfer the chickpeas to a large mixing bowl and add the flax mixture and mashed sweet potatoes. Add the remaining kofta ingredients and mix thoroughly. If the mixture is too dry to hold together, add a little water (a tablespoon at a time) until moistened.

6. Form the mixture into small balls and place them on the prepared baking sheet. Bake for 20 to 30 minutes, until golden brown.

7. Meanwhile, to make the malai sauce, combine the cashews, water, coconut milk, cornstarch, curry powder, garam masala, cumin, red pepper flakes, tomato paste, and maple syrup in a high-powered blender and puree until smooth. Set aside.

8. In a large saucepan over medium-high heat, sauté the onion, garlic, and ginger in a small amount of water until tender, about 8 minutes. Add the sauce from the blender, reduce the heat to medium, and simmer until bubbly and thickened, about 5 minutes.

9. Add the remaining sauce ingredients and mix thoroughly. Reduce the heat to low and simmer for 10 minutes.

10. When the kofta balls are done, add them to the sauce. Serve warm.

Pad Thai

Most restaurants serve pad thai with an oil-based fish sauce. My version is oil-free and plant-based but still boasts that delicious combination of sweet, sour, and spicy flavors.

Sauce

2 garlic cloves, peeled

1 teaspoon grated fresh ginger

¼ cup water

3 tablespoons low-sodium tamari

2 tablespoons pure maple syrup

1 tablespoon rice vinegar

1 tablespoon tahini

1 tablespoon lime juice

1 teaspoon tamarind paste

1 teaspoon sriracha

2 teaspoons cornstarch

Noodles and Vegetables

6 ounces extra-firm tofu

6 to 8 ounces brown rice noodles

1 medium carrot, peeled and julienned

1 red bell pepper, seeded and sliced

½ red onion, sliced

3 cups chopped broccoli florets

1 cup shredded cabbage

2 cups chopped spinach

1 cup fresh mung bean sprouts

4 to 6 green onions, chopped

3 to 5 garlic cloves, minced

Toppings

½ cup chopped peanuts

½ cup chopped fresh cilantro

1 lime, cut into wedges (optional)

Yields: 4 to 6 servings
Prep Time: 25 minutes
Cook Time: 30 minutes

1. Preheat the oven to 400°F. Line a baking sheet with parchment paper.

2. Combine all the sauce ingredients in a blender and blend until smooth and creamy.

3. Cut the tofu into 1-inch cubes and arrange them in a single layer on the prepared baking sheet. Brush the tofu thoroughly with the sauce (reserve the remaining sauce for the vegetables). Bake until golden, 15 to 20 minutes.

4. While the tofu is baking, cook the rice noodles according to the package instructions. Drain and set aside.

5. In a nonstick skillet over medium-high heat, sauté the carrot, bell pepper, red onion, broccoli, cabbage, spinach, sprouts, green onions, and garlic in a small amount of water until the broccoli is bright and tender, about 5 to 8 minutes. Add the reserved sauce and continue cooking until the sauce thickens, about 3 minutes.

6. In a large serving bowl, toss the pasta, tofu, and vegetables together. Garnish with the peanuts and cilantro and serve with the lime wedges, if desired.

- Don't hesitate to try different veggies in this dish. I like the variety and color of the ones I use here, but you can choose your own favorites.
- Tamarind paste (a sticky sour fruit paste) can be found in the Asian section of most large supermarkets; Whole Foods Market carries this product as well. But if you can't find it, you can substitute 1 pitted date.

Peanutty Greens and Tofu

The idea for this delicious and fun recipe was inspired by one of my favorite cookbook authors, Isa Chandra Moskowitz (author of *Veganomicon* and *Isa Does It*). I love a creamy curried peanut sauce and often double this sauce recipe so I can use it on other vegetables throughout the week. There are so many flavors and textures in this recipe; it is truly one of my favorites!

Sauce

1 cup water

⅓ cup all-natural peanut butter (100% peanuts)

2 tablespoons rice vinegar

2 tablespoons pure maple syrup

2 teaspoons low-sodium tamari

1 teaspoon sriracha

1 tablespoon grated fresh ginger

2 teaspoons curry powder

1 tablespoon cornstarch

Tofu and Vegetables

1 (14-ounce) package extra-firm tofu

1 bunch kale, stemmed and chopped

2 or 3 carrots, peeled and shredded

1 red bell pepper, seeded and sliced

½ red onion, diced

1 celery stalk, sliced

6 cups cooked brown rice, for serving

½ cup chopped fresh cilantro, for garnish

½ cup chopped peanuts, for garnish

Yields: 4 servings
Prep Time: 30 minutes, plus 1 hour to marinate
Cook Time: 30 minutes

1. In a large mixing bowl, whisk together all the sauce ingredients. Blending it in a blender helps emulsify ingredients and creates a creamier texture.

2. Cut the tofu into triangles. Put the tofu in the peanut sauce and set aside to marinate for 1 hour.

3. Preheat the oven to 400°F. Line a baking sheet with parchment paper.

4. Place the marinated tofu in a single layer on the prepared baking sheet. Reserve the sauce for the vegetables. Bake for 15 minutes, turn the tofu over, and continue baking for an additional 15 to 20 minutes. The tofu should become dry and slightly golden around the edges.

5. While the tofu is baking, in a large nonstick skillet over medium-high heat, sauté the kale, carrots, bell pepper, onion, and celery in a small amount of water until crisp-tender, about 5 minutes. Add the reserved sauce to the skillet and stir to combine it with the vegetables. Cook over medium heat until the sauce thickens.

6. Serve the kale mixture over the brown rice, with the grilled tofu on the side. Garnish with the cilantro and peanuts.

Potato-Crusted Mushroom Quiche

I love quiche but often struggle with the rich, fatty crusts that go with them. This quiche has a shredded potato crust that is light and delicious. It's perfect for breakfast or dinner!

Crust

2 tablespoons flax meal or chia seeds

6 tablespoons water

2 or 3 large russet potatoes

1 teaspoon garlic powder

1 teaspoon onion powder

Sea salt

Black pepper

Filling

1 onion, chopped

3 garlic cloves, minced

8 ounces button mushrooms, sliced

4 ounces shiitake mushrooms, sliced

¼ cup chopped fresh parsley

1 tablespoon chopped fresh thyme

1 tablespoon chopped fresh rosemary

1 (14-ounce) package extra-firm tofu

¼ cup nutritional yeast flakes

½ teaspoon sea salt

¼ teaspoon black pepper

2 tomatoes, thinly sliced

Yields: 4 servings
Prep Time: 30 minutes
Cook Time: 1 hour

1. Preheat the oven to 375°F. Line a 10-inch pie pan with parchment paper.

2. In a small bowl, combine the flax meal and water. Set aside to thicken.

3. Peel and shred the potatoes with the shredding blade of a food processor or by hand with a box grater. Rinse the potato shreds and pat dry. Transfer to a bowl and add the flax mixture, garlic powder, and onion powder. Mix thoroughly.

4. Pat the shredded potatoes into the prepared pie pan, making sure to cover the entire bottom and sides. Season with salt and pepper to taste. Bake for 10 to 15 minutes, until the potatoes begin to brown. Set aside to cool.

5. In a nonstick skillet over medium-high heat, sauté the onion, garlic, mushrooms, parsley, thyme, and rosemary in a small amount of water until tender, about 8 minutes. Remove from the heat.

6. Combine the tofu, nutritional yeast, salt, and pepper in a food processor or blender and blend until smooth and creamy. Transfer to a mixing bowl and add the sautéed vegetables. Mix thoroughly.

7. Spread the tofu-mushroom mixture over the potato crust in the pie pan. Top with the tomato slices.

8. Bake for 40 minutes, or until firmly set. Let stand for 10 to 15 minutes, then cut into wedges to serve.

Scalloped Potatoes

I have always loved scalloped potatoes; my mother makes a wonderful traditional version that was my favorite feel-good dinner as a kid. Even as an adult, this is the dinner I request from my mother most. These days I ask her to leave out the ham and substitute a plant-based milk, but it's still my definition of comfort food. Thanks, Mom!

Sauce

- 2½ cups unsweetened plant-based milk
- 2 teaspoons lemon juice
- 1 teaspoon Dijon mustard
- ¼ cup whole wheat flour
- 3 tablespoons nutritional yeast flakes
- 1 teaspoon garlic powder
- 1 teaspoon onion powder
- ½ teaspoon ground turmeric
- ¾ teaspoon sea salt
- ½ teaspoon black pepper

Potatoes

- 2 pounds russet potatoes (about 6 medium), peeled and cut into ¼-inch-thick slices
- 2 onions, cut into ¼-inch-thick slices
- ¼ cup chopped fresh parsley
- ¼ teaspoon smoked paprika

Yields: 4 to 6 servings
Prep Time: 30 minutes
Cook Time: 50 minutes

1. Preheat the oven to 375°F. Line a 9- by 13-inch baking dish with parchment paper.

2. Combine all the sauce ingredients in a blender and puree until smooth.

3. Arrange half of the potato slices and half of the onion slices in an overlapping layer in the prepared baking dish. Sprinkle with the parsley, and then pour half of the milk sauce over the potatoes and onions. Repeat with the remaining potatoes, onions, parsley, and sauce. Sprinkle the paprika over the top.

4. Cover the dish with aluminum foil and bake for 30 minutes. Uncover and cook for 15 more minutes, or until the top is golden and bubbly. Serve warm.

Kim's Hints:

- *If you have a mandoline, that will allow you to get perfectly uniform potato slices.*
- *You can parboil the potato slices for 10 to 12 minutes before assembly in order to reduce the baking time.*

Potato Veggie Enchiladas

These enchiladas might seem like a little more work than other recipes, but if you make them when you already have leftover mashed potatoes, you can skip the first step in the directions. (My college kids have even made these with instant mashed potatoes; just be sure to read the ingredients list carefully to make sure there's no milk in the brand you buy.) You can use your favorite commercial enchilada sauce (be sure to check the label for oil) or make your own (see page 96).

4 medium russet potatoes, peeled and quartered

½ cup unsweetened plant-based milk

2 tablespoons nutritional yeast flakes

1 onion, diced

1 poblano pepper, seeded and minced

8 ounces spinach, fresh or frozen, chopped

1 cup corn, fresh or frozen

2 teaspoons chili powder

1 teaspoon ground cumin

1 teaspoon garlic powder

½ teaspoon sea salt

½ teaspoon black pepper

3 cups Enchilada Sauce (page 96)

12 corn tortillas

1 avocado, pitted, peeled, and diced, for garnish (optional)

Yields: 4 to 6 servings
Prep Time: 30 minutes
Cook Time: 40 minutes

1. Preheat the oven to 375°F.

2. Put the potatoes in a medium saucepan and add enough cold water to cover. Bring to a boil over medium-high heat and cook until tender, about 15 minutes. Drain the potatoes, return them to the saucepan, and mash them with the milk and nutritional yeast. Set aside.

3. Meanwhile, in a large nonstick skillet over medium-high heat, sauté the onion, poblano pepper, spinach, corn, chili powder, cumin, garlic powder, salt, and pepper in a small amount of water until vegetables are tender, about 10 minutes.

4. Spoon 1 cup of the enchilada sauce into the bottom of a 9- by 13-inch baking dish. Spread a layer of mashed potatoes on each corn tortilla and top with spoonful of sautéed veggies. Roll up each enchilada and arrange them in the baking dish, seam side down. Spoon the remaining enchilada sauce over the enchiladas and bake for 20 minutes. Let the enchiladas cool a bit, then garnish with the avocado, if desired, and serve.

Kim's Hint: *If you've filled all your corn tortillas and have extra vegetable filling leftover, just spread it around the edges of the baking dish and top with sauce.*

Shepherd's Pie

Shepherd's pie is basically mashed potatoes with a very hearty gravy stew. For this recipe, I started with the flavors from our vegan mushroom gravy and added my favorite vegetables. This recipe can also be made and baked in individual oven-safe bowls for serving ease.

Mashed Potatoes

3 pounds russet potatoes, peeled and chopped

¾ cup unsweetened plant-based milk

¼ cup nutritional yeast flakes

2 teaspoons chopped fresh chives

½ teaspoon sea salt

¼ teaspoon black pepper

½ teaspoon paprika

Vegetable Filling

1 cup low-sodium vegetable broth or water

1 tablespoon tomato paste

2 teaspoons vegan Worcestershire sauce

2 tablespoons whole wheat flour

2 teaspoons Italian herb blend

½ teaspoon sea salt

¼ teaspoon black pepper

2 medium onions, sliced

2 carrots, peeled and diced

2 celery stalks, sliced

4 garlic cloves, minced

4 medium portobello mushroom caps, sliced

½ cup dry red wine

1 cup corn, fresh or frozen

1 cup peas, fresh or frozen

Yields: 6 servings
Prep Time: 30 minutes
Cook Time: 40 minutes

1. Preheat the oven to 375°F.

2. Put the potatoes in a medium saucepan and add enough cold water to cover. Bring to a boil over medium-high heat and cook until tender, about 15 minutes. Drain the potatoes and transfer them to a large bowl. Add the milk, nutritional yeast, chives, salt, and pepper. Using a hand-held mixer, puree the potatoes until smooth and creamy.

3. In a small bowl, whisk together the vegetable broth, tomato paste, Worcestershire sauce, whole wheat flour, Italian herb blend, salt, and pepper. Set aside.

4. In a nonstick skillet over medium heat, sauté the onions, carrots, celery, and garlic in a small amount of water until tender, about 8 minutes. Add the mushrooms and wine and sauté until the mushrooms are tender, about 5 minutes. Add the corn, peas, and broth mixture. Cook over medium heat until thickened, about 5 minutes.

5. Transfer the vegetable mixture to a 9- by 13-inch baking dish lined with parchment paper. Spoon the mashed potatoes evenly over the vegetables. Sprinkle the paprika over the top. Bake for 15 minutes, or until the potatoes are evenly browned. Serve warm.

Slow Cooker Jackfruit Tacos

Jackfruit has become increasingly popular in vegan restaurants, and I couldn't publish another cookbook without sharing a fun jackfruit recipe. When cooked, it has the texture and appearance of pulled pork. It also absorbs flavors beautifully. This Mexican-style jackfruit is one you won't want to skip if you're serving tacos or building a hearty burrito.

1 onion, diced

1 green bell pepper, seeded and diced

1 poblano pepper, seeded and diced

2 (20-ounce) cans green jackfruit, rinsed and drained

1½ cups favorite salsa verde (green tomatillo salsa) or red salsa

1 tablespoon chili powder

2 teaspoons garlic powder

1 teaspoon smoked paprika

⅛ teaspoon red pepper flakes (optional)

8 to 10 corn or whole-grain flour tortillas

Toppings

3 to 4 cups mixed greens

1 avocado, pitted, peeled, and diced

2 cups favorite salsa

3 green onions, sliced

Yields: 4 to 6 servings
Prep Time: 20 minutes
Cook Time: 4 to 6 hours

1. Combine the onion, bell pepper, poblano, jackfruit, salsa, chili powder, garlic powder, paprika, and red pepper flakes (if using) in a slow cooker. Cover and cook on high for 3 to 4 hours.

2. When you are nearly ready to serve, preheat the oven to 300°F. Wrap the tortillas in aluminum foil and heat in the oven while you prepare the toppings.

3. With two forks, gently pull apart the jackfruit until it has the appearance of pulled pork. Turn down the heat to low and cover until you are ready to serve.

4. Serve the warm tortillas topped with jackfruit filling, greens, avocado, salsa, and green onions.

Kim's Hints:

- *I prefer Trader Joe's corn tortillas, which are a blend of wheat and corn. They are softer and healthier than any I've seen in other stores and are a great option if you can have gluten.*
- *When we have tacos, I like to offer a variety of fillings such as corn, black olives, cilantro, pico de gallo, black beans, guacamole, and Spicy Nacho Sauce (page 140). There is no limit to what I will put in a taco!*

Smoky Beans

Nelson and I had the best vegan smoky beans ever at a small pub in Hillsborough, North Carolina. Of course, then my challenge was to create my own version that would be every bit as flavorful. Luckily, it came together quickly, and I hit upon the perfect combination of smoky ingredients. The secret to achieving the right texture is to puree half of the beans.

3 celery stalks, diced

2 carrots, peeled and diced

1 onion, diced

1 poblano pepper, seeded and diced

2 tablespoons minced garlic

2 (15-ounce) cans red kidney beans, rinsed and drained, or 3 cups cooked red kidney beans, divided

1 (15-ounce) can diced tomatoes, undrained

2 teaspoons minced chipotle peppers in adobo sauce

½ cup low-sodium vegetable broth, or more if needed

2 teaspoons apple cider vinegar

1 teaspoon molasses

½ teaspoon liquid smoke

1 tablespoon smoked paprika

2 teaspoons onion powder

1 teaspoon dried thyme

1 teaspoon dried oregano

½ teaspoon sea salt

¼ teaspoon black pepper

Yields: 6 servings
Prep Time: 20 minutes
Cook Time: 30 minutes

1. In a large saucepan over medium-high heat, sauté the celery, carrots, onion, poblano pepper, and garlic in a small amount of water until tender, about 8 minutes.

2. Combine 1 can of red beans and the diced tomatoes with their juices in a blender and blend until smooth and creamy. Transfer this mixture to the pan with the sautéed vegetables. Stir in the remaining 1 can of whole beans.

3. Add the remaining ingredients, reduce the heat to low, and simmer for 20 to 30 minutes. If you prefer a thinner consistency, add more vegetable broth, a tablespoon at a time. Serve warm.

Southwestern Chili Mac

The combination of chili, pasta, and cheesy sauce makes this a great kid-friendly recipe. The sauce is made with butternut squash and cashews, which gives it a slightly sweet flavor.

Sauce

1 cup mashed cooked butternut squash

1 jalapeño, seeded and coarsely chopped

¼ cup raw cashews

1½ cups unsweetened plant-based milk

1½ teaspoons lemon juice

¼ cup nutritional yeast flakes

2 tablespoons cornstarch

2 teaspoons chili powder

1 teaspoon garlic powder

1 teaspoon smoked paprika

1 teaspoon sea salt

Chili Mac

12 ounces whole-grain elbow macaroni

1 (15-ounce) can black beans, rinsed and drained, or 1½ cups cooked black beans

1 red bell pepper, seeded and diced

1 cup corn, frozen or fresh

9 green onions, sliced, divided

½ cup panko bread crumbs

Yields: 6 servings
Prep Time: 20 minutes
Cook Time: 40 minutes

1. Preheat the oven to 350°F.

2. Combine all the sauce ingredients in a high-powered blender and blend until smooth and creamy. Transfer the mixture to a saucepan and whisk over medium heat until thickened, about 5 minutes. If you prefer a thinner consistency, add a tablespoon or two of water. Set aside.

3. Cook the macaroni according to the package instructions. Drain the macaroni and transfer it to a large mixing bowl. Add the black beans, bell pepper, corn, two-thirds of the green onions, and the cheese sauce. Mix well to combine.

4. Transfer the mixture to a casserole dish lined with parchment paper and sprinkle the panko bread crumbs all over the top. Bake for 20 to 30 minutes, until golden brown and bubbly. Garnish with the remaining green onions and serve.

Kim's Hints:

- *Using frozen mashed butternut squash is a huge time saver here. You can also try using frozen (or freshly cooked) mashed sweet potatoes for a slightly different flavor.*
- *We love topping this dish with salsa for additional Mexican flavor.*

Spicy Tahini Stir-Fry

This powerhouse stir-fry is packed with vegetables and soba noodles, but it's the sauce that makes it extra special. Sriracha provides the heat in this dish; feel free to scale it up or down to your preference.

8 ounces soba noodles

Sauce

¼ cup water

3 tablespoons tahini

2 tablespoons Hoisin Sauce (page 97)

1 tablespoon apple cider vinegar

1 tablespoon low-sodium tamari

1 tablespoon sriracha, or to taste

2 garlic cloves, peeled

1 tablespoon grated fresh ginger

¼ teaspoon ground turmeric

Vegetables

1 bunch kale, stemmed and chopped

1 carrot, peeled and julienned

1 cup sliced red cabbage

1 cup frozen edamame, thawed

1 red bell pepper, seeded and sliced

8 ounces shiitake or other mushrooms, sliced

2 tablespoons sesame seeds, for garnish

Yields: 4 servings
Prep Time: 20 minutes
Cook Time: 15 minutes

1. Cook the soba noodles according to the package instructions. Drain the noodles and set aside.

2. Combine all the sauce ingredients in a blender and blend on high until smooth and creamy.

3. In a large nonstick skillet over medium-high heat, sauté the kale, carrot, cabbage, edamame, bell pepper, and mushrooms in a small amount of water until slightly wilted and tender, about 8 minutes. Add the sauce to the vegetables and stir to mix.

4. Serve the vegetables and sauce over the soba noodles, garnished with the sesame seeds.

Kim's Hint: *I love soba noodles for their strongly nutty flavor, but you can use any type of whole-grain pasta in this recipe.*

Stuffed Acorn Squash

When I was growing up, my mother used to bake acorn squash with a pinch of brown sugar, salt, and pepper. It's my favorite fall dish! I've added a few more flavors and textures in this recipe, and it only gets better. Try to find in-season organic squash, since it is usually much sweeter than conventionally grown squash.

2 medium acorn squash, halved lengthwise and seeded

1 tablespoon fennel seeds

1 large leek, white and green parts only, halved lengthwise and thinly sliced crosswise

4 garlic cloves, minced

4 cups finely chopped kale

½ cup low-sodium vegetable broth

7 ounces extra-firm tofu, crumbled

½ cup chopped walnuts

3 tablespoons nutritional yeast flakes, divided

½ cup whole wheat bread crumbs, divided

1 teaspoon onion powder

½ teaspoon sea salt

½ teaspoon black pepper

¼ teaspoon smoked paprika, for garnish

Yields: 4 servings
Prep Time: 40 minutes
Cook Time: 1 hour

1. Preheat the oven to 400°F. Line a baking sheet pan with parchment paper.

2. Place the squash halves cut-side down on the prepared baking sheet. Bake until tender, 40 to 45 minutes. Remove from the oven, turn the squash over, and set aside.

3. In a large nonstick skillet over high heat, dry-toast the fennel seeds until golden. Transfer the seeds to a plate.

4. In the same skillet, sauté the leek, garlic, and kale in the vegetable broth over medium-high heat. When the vegetables are tender, stir in the crumbled tofu, walnuts, 2 tablespoons of the nutritional yeast, ¼ cup of the bread crumbs, the toasted fennel seeds, onion powder, salt, and pepper.

5. Divide the vegetable filling among the four squash halves. Sprinkle with the remaining 1 tablespoon nutritional yeast and ¼ cup bread crumbs. Bake for 20 to 30 minutes, until the edges are golden brown. Sprinkle on the smoked paprika and serve.

Stuffed Bell Peppers

Our PlantPure Nation health coach, Laura Dietrich, shared this recipe with me and it's delicious. Stuffed peppers were a family favorite when I was a kid. This version replaces the hamburger and cheese with beans and grains. These stuffed peppers are even better as leftovers—they absorb more flavor but still hold their shape after being cooled and reheated.

4 bell peppers (any colors)

1 cup cooked brown rice

1 (15-ounce) can black beans, rinsed and drained, or 1½ cups cooked black beans

1 cup corn, fresh or frozen

1 cup mild salsa, divided

1 tablespoon nutritional yeast flakes

2 teaspoons chili powder

1 teaspoon ground cumin

1 teaspoon garlic powder

Yields: 4 servings
Prep Time: 15 minutes
Cook Time: 45 minutes

1. Preheat the oven to 375°F.

2. Slice off the top of each bell pepper (reserve the tops) and remove the seeds and ribs inside.

3. In a medium bowl, combine the brown rice, black beans, corn, ½ cup of the salsa, nutritional yeast flakes, chili powder, cumin, and garlic powder and mix until thoroughly blended. Stuff the peppers with the rice filling.

4. Spread the remaining ½ cup salsa in the bottom of a small casserole dish. Place the stuffed peppers in the casserole, top each pepper with its reserved "hat," cover with aluminum foil, and bake for 30 minutes.

5. Turn the oven up to 425°F. Remove the foil covering and bake for an additional 15 minutes. Serve warm.

Kim's Hint: *The Spicy Nacho Sauce (page 140) makes a nice addition to this recipe. Pour it over the peppers before serving.*

Stuffed Cabbage

Stuffed cabbage is a classic comfort food traditionally made with beef or pork, but I think you'll find that this plant-based version is just as delicious. Although this recipe is a bit time-consuming, the effort is well worth it. It can be made several days ahead of time and seems to develop better flavor with each hour and day that passes. It goes perfectly with mashed potatoes on a cold winter night.

Glaze

1 (15-ounce) can crushed tomatoes

¼ cup tomato paste

1 tablespoon molasses

1 tablespoon Dijon mustard

1 tablespoon low-sodium tamari

¼ teaspoon ground allspice

Stuffed Cabbage

2 tablespoons flax meal or chia seeds

¼ cup water

1 head cabbage, cored

1 onion, quartered

2 carrots, peeled and quartered

1 green or red bell pepper, seeded and quartered

3 celery stalks, quartered

3 garlic cloves, peeled

¾ cup walnuts

1 (15-ounce) can chickpeas, rinsed and drained, or 1½ cups cooked chickpeas

2 tablespoons vegan Worcestershire sauce

1 cup oats

1 cup cooked brown rice

2 tablespoons chili powder

1 teaspoon dried oregano

½ teaspoon sea salt

¼ teaspoon black pepper

Yields: 6 servings
Prep Time: 45 minutes
Cook Time: 35 minutes

1. Preheat the oven to 375°F. Line an 8-inch square baking dish with parchment paper.

2. In a medium bowl, combine all the glaze ingredients and mix well. Set aside.

3. In a small bowl, combine the flax meal and water. Set aside to thicken.

4. In a large saucepan, bring 3 or 4 inches of water to a boil over high heat. Put the cabbage in the water, cored-side down, cover the pan, and reduce the heat to low. Steam the cabbage for 20 minutes, or until the leaves pull apart easily. Using tongs, remove the leaves as they cook and put them in a colander. You will need to do this throughout the cooking process until you have 14 to 16 leaves that are ready for stuffing. Set aside.

5. In a food processor, combine the onion, carrots, bell pepper, celery, garlic, and walnuts. Process until the vegetables and nuts are coarsely chopped. Add the chickpeas and continue processing until they are coarsely ground.

6. Transfer the vegetable mixture to a large bowl and add the flax mixture, Worcestershire sauce, oats, brown rice, chili powder, oregano, salt, and black pepper.

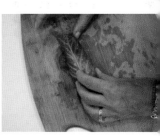

Mix thoroughly. If the mixture does not have the consistency of meatloaf, add water, a tablespoon at a time, until the mixture is moist and holds together well.

7. Spread half of the tomato glaze mixture in the bottom of the prepared baking dish.

8. Lay out each cabbage leaf and spoon ½ to ¾ cup of the vegetable mixture onto the leaf (the amount will depend on the size of the leaf). Don't overload them because you will need room to wrap them up. Fold in the two sides and roll up like a burrito. Place each cabbage wrap, seam-side down, in the baking dish.

9. Drizzle a small amount of the tomato glaze over each wrap.

10. Bake for 30 to 35 minutes, until the tomato glaze is caramelized. Let the cabbage wraps stand for 15 to 20 minutes before serving.

Kim's Hints:

- If you have leftover cabbage after you remove the leaves you need for this recipe, you can slice it up and add it to a stir-fry or mix it into mashed potatoes.
- Instead of brown rice, you can use cooked quinoa or couscous, or whole wheat bread crumbs.

Sweet Mayan Lasagna

Sometimes I don't have time to roll enchiladas or burritos, so I make a casserole or a lasagna-style dish instead. During PlantPure Nation's first Jumpstart program in North Carolina, we had so many sweet potatoes and beans left over that we came up with this highly requested dish. The filling can be created from whatever vegetables and beans you have on hand, though I really enjoy the combination of the original.

3 sweet potatoes, peeled and quartered

2 tablespoons nutritional yeast flakes

¼ teaspoon chipotle chile powder

Sea salt

1 (15-ounce) can black beans, rinsed and drained, or 1½ cups cooked black beans

1 red onion, diced

1 poblano pepper, seeded and diced

1 cup chopped mango, fresh or frozen

2 cups corn, fresh or frozen

1 tablespoon lime juice

1 tablespoon low-sodium tamari

2 tablespoons chili powder

½ teaspoon ground cumin

⅛ teaspoon red pepper flakes

4 cups salsa, divided

18 corn tortillas

¼ cup raw pumpkin seeds

Yields: 4 to 6 servings
Prep Time: 20 minutes
Cook Time: 35 minutes

1. Preheat the oven to 375°F. Line a 9- by 13-inch baking dish with parchment paper.

2. Bring a medium saucepan of water to a boil over medium-high heat. Add the sweet potatoes and cook for 10 to 15 minutes, until the potatoes are tender when poked with a fork. Drain the sweet potatoes and transfer them to a medium bowl. Mash the sweet potatoes with the nutritional yeast and chipotle chile powder until smooth and creamy. Season with salt to taste. Set aside.

3. In a large mixing bowl, combine the beans, red onion, poblano pepper, mango chunks, corn, lime juice, tamari, chili powder, cumin, and red pepper flakes. Mix until well blended but take care not to smash the beans. Set aside.

4. Spread 1 cup of the salsa in the bottom of the prepared baking dish. Cover the salsa with 6 tortillas, overlapping them as needed to fit. Add layers in the following order: half of the mashed sweet potatoes, half of the black bean mixture, and 1 cup of salsa. Repeat the layers using 6 more tortillas, the remaining sweet potatoes, the remaining black beans, and 1 more cup of salsa. Add one last layer of 6 corn tortillas and top with the remaining 1 cup salsa. Scatter the pumpkin seeds over the top.

5. Cover the lasagna with aluminum foil and bake for 20 minutes. Remove the foil and bake for another 10 to 15 minutes. Set the lasagna aside to cool for 10 to 15 minutes before serving.

Kim's Hints:

- Instead of cooking the sweet potatoes yourself, you can save time by using 4 cups frozen mashed sweet potatoes (thawed).
- You can use flour tortillas instead of corn, though it makes for a slightly denser casserole.
- I often add a layer of spinach for a few extra nutrients.
- Try serving this lasagna topped with diced avocados, sliced green onions, and a dollop of plant-based sour cream.
- I like to buy corn tortillas from Trader Joe's because they don't fall apart like traditional corn tortillas, and they have a healthy ingredient list. I prefer the consistency of their tortillas in this casserole.

Sweet Potato Moussaka

This recipe takes a little extra time, but it's well worth it. It's perfect for a large dinner crowd since it can be made ahead of time. The longer it sits after baking, the better it tastes. I love the warm flavors of cinnamon and allspice combined with the heartiness of potatoes and lentils. Serve this dish with a green salad and warm bread and you'll have a winning meal!

Vegetables

2 medium eggplant, peeled and cut lengthwise into ¼-inch-thick slices

Sea salt

2 medium sweet potatoes, peeled and cut lengthwise into ¼-inch-thick slices

Red Sauce

1 onion, halved then thinly sliced

6 garlic cloves, minced

⅓ cup dry red wine

1 (28-ounce) can crushed tomatoes

1½ cups cooked lentils

1 tablespoon agave nectar

1 bay leaf

2 teaspoons Italian herb blend

½ teaspoon ground cinnamon

¼ teaspoon ground allspice

¼ teaspoon red pepper flakes

½ teaspoon sea salt

Cashew-Tofu Cream

1 (14-ounce) package extra-firm tofu

¼ cup raw cashews

1 cup water

2 tablespoons lemon juice

2 garlic cloves, peeled

2 dates, pitted

2 tablespoons nutritional yeast flakes

⅛ teaspoon ground nutmeg

½ teaspoon sea salt

¼ teaspoon black pepper

1 cup whole wheat bread crumbs

Yields: 4 to 6 servings
Prep Time: 40 minutes
Cook Time: 90 minutes

1. Preheat the oven to 400°F. Line two baking sheets with parchment paper. Also line a 9- by 13-inch baking dish with parchment paper.

2. Rub the eggplant slices with a little salt and set aside in a colander in the sink for about 15 minutes to soften, then briefly rinse with cold water.

3. Lay out the eggplant and sweet potato slices in a single layer on the prepared baking sheets. Roast for 15 to 20 minutes, until tender. Set aside to cool.

4. While the vegetables are roasting, prepare the tomato sauce. In a medium saucepan set over medium-high heat, sauté the onion and garlic in the red wine until tender and slightly reduced, 2 to 3 minutes. Add the crushed tomatoes, lentils, agave nectar, bay

leaf, Italian herb blend, cinnamon, allspice, and red pepper flakes. Reduce the heat to medium-low, cover, and simmer for 15 to 20 minutes, stirring occasionally. The sauce will reduce slightly. Turn off the heat, remove the bay leaf, and add the salt.

5. In a food processor or high-powered blender, blend the tofu, cashews, water, lemon juice, garlic, dates, nutritional yeast, nutmeg, salt, and black pepper until you have a smooth, creamy mixture.

6. Spread ½ cup of the tomato-lentil sauce in the bottom of the prepared baking dish. Add layers in the following order: half of the eggplant slices, half of the tofu cream, half of the sweet potato slices, half of the remaining tomato sauce, and half of the bread crumbs. Repeat the layers with the remaining ingredients.

7. Cover the baking dish with aluminum foil and bake for 1 hour. Remove the foil and bake for an additional 10 to 15 minutes. Cool the moussaka for 20 to 30 minutes before serving.

Vegetable Stew with Dumplings

This was always a highly requested meal when my kids were young. It's a delicious one-pot meal that can be prepared quickly: lots of vegetables, a little pasta, and moist dumplings that pull it all together.

1 onion, diced

1 red bell pepper, seeded and diced

2 celery stalks, diced

2 carrots, peeled and diced

1 large potato, peeled and diced

1½ cups water

3 cups low-sodium vegetable broth

½ cup whole-grain orzo

2 (15-ounce) cans cannellini beans, rinsed and drained, or 3 cups cooked cannellini beans

2 cups frozen peas

1 teaspoon ground mustard

¾ teaspoon sea salt

½ teaspoon black pepper

Dumplings

1 cup whole wheat pastry flour

⅔ cup finely ground cornmeal

1½ teaspoons baking powder

2 teaspoons dried dill

¼ teaspoon sea salt

1 cup unsweetened plant-based milk

1 tablespoon pure maple syrup

Yields: 4 servings
Prep Time: 30 minutes
Cook Time: 35 minutes

1. In a large saucepan over medium-high heat, sauté the onion, bell pepper, celery, carrots, and potato in the water until the onion is tender, about 8 minutes.

2. Add the vegetable broth and bring to a boil. Add the whole wheat orzo, beans, frozen peas, mustard, salt, and black pepper. Reduce the heat to medium and simmer, stirring frequently, for 10 to 15 minutes, until the potatoes are tender and the orzo is fully cooked. Reduce the heat to low.

3. To make the dumplings, whisk together the flour, cornmeal, baking powder, dill, and salt. Add the milk and maple syrup and stir only until moistened; do not overmix.

4. Gently drop the dumpling dough by rounded tablespoon into the simmering stew. Cook for 10 minutes. Cover the pan and continue cooking for another 10 minutes. Serve warm.

Welsh Rarebit

When I was in elementary school, our school cafeteria made this dish. That was almost 40 years ago, and I clearly remember the cafeteria workers actually cooking the meals behind the scenes as opposed to microwaving fried foods as they often do in today's school cafeterias. Obviously the old English version of this recipe isn't healthy, but this plant-based version still brings back fond memories from my childhood.

1 cup raw cashews

2 cups water

1 teaspoon cornstarch

¾ cup beer (any variety, including nonalcoholic)

1 tablespoon tahini

2 teaspoons Dijon mustard

1 teaspoon lemon juice

1 teaspoon white miso

1 teaspoon vegan Worcestershire sauce

¼ cup nutritional yeast flakes

1 teaspoon onion powder

½ teaspoon garlic powder

¼ teaspoon sea salt

⅛ teaspoon cayenne pepper

6 slices whole-grain bread, toasted

2 tomatoes, sliced

Yields: 4 servings
Prep Time: 30 minutes
Cook Time: 15 minutes

1. Combine the cashews, water, and cornstarch in a high-powered blender and blend until smooth. Set aside.

2. In a medium saucepan set over medium heat, whisk together the beer, tahini, Dijon mustard, lemon juice, miso, Worcestershire sauce, nutritional yeast, onion powder, garlic powder, salt, and cayenne. Cook until the ingredients are completely combined and the mixture begins to steam.

3. Whisk the blended cashew cream into the beer mixture and cook, stirring often, until you have a smooth sauce. It will take 7 to 10 minutes to get the sauce bubbly and completely thickened.

4. Slice the toast diagonally to make triangles. Arrange the toast points on plates and then pour the sauce over the toast. Top with sliced tomatoes and serve.

Sides

Plant-Based Holidays

As a plant-based eater, a common question you'll receive around the holidays is, "But what do you eat?" In truth, a plant-based holiday meal is often substantively more diverse than traditional American holiday meals, with a wide variety of flavors, colors, and textures.

A tradition we and many others follow around holiday times is to include everyone in the cooking process. Often dinner guests are given a category and asked to create or find a recipe within that category—for example, a bread, salad, or dessert. It makes the meal more interesting and fun when everyone is part of the cooking process. It's the memory around the meal, not just the meal, that is important to create.

You also should consider experimenting with new traditions and habits that can become part of your family tradition. If Christmas Eve used to be all about seafood, maybe it can become plant-based with sea flavors such as fishless sticks, zucchini cakes, New England chowder, or linguine with plant-based Alfredo sauce rather than clams (all recipes you can find in the PlantPure cookbooks!).

I'm not sure if Super Bowl Sunday is technically a holiday, but I think one could almost consider it a "junk food" holiday. Yet there are so many healthy recipes suited for the occasion; in this book alone you can find Spicy Nacho Sauce (page 140), Layered Taco Salad Dip (page 136), Slow Cooker Jackfruit Tacos (page 197), Carrot Dogs (page 71), Baked Salt and Vinegar Fries (page 230), and much more.

Healthy holiday eating is all about changing your mind-set. Think plants!

A plate from the Campbells' Thanksgiving

Scalloped Corn

This is always the first dish that is devoured at our Thanksgiving dinner. The corn gives it a mildly sweet yet savory flavor.

1 onion, diced

2 green bell peppers, seeded and diced

¼ cup low-sodium vegetable broth

2 cups unsweetened plant-based milk

6 tablespoons whole wheat flour

½ teaspoon ground mustard

½ teaspoon smoked paprika

½ teaspoon black pepper

⅛ teaspoon ground nutmeg

6 cups corn, fresh or frozen (thawed)

¼ cup whole wheat bread crumbs

Yields: 6 servings
Prep Time: 15 minutes
Cook Time: 30 minutes

1. Preheat the oven to 375°F.

2. In a medium saucepan over medium-high heat, sauté the onion and bell peppers in the vegetable broth until tender, about 8 minutes.

3. In a small bowl, whisk together the milk, flour, mustard powder, paprika, black pepper, and nutmeg until all the lumps are gone.

4. In a large mixing bowl, combine the corn, sautéed vegetables, and milk mixture and mix well. Scoop into a 9-inch square baking dish. Sprinkle with the bread crumbs and bake for 30 minutes, or until the top is bubbly and golden brown. Serve warm.

Mustard-Glazed Potatoes and Kale

This sweet mustard sauce adds so much flavor to simple potatoes and greens that it becomes the perfect dish to pass around the holiday table. It's colorful, starchy, and full of flavor.

1 pound red potatoes, cubed

1 onion, chopped

5 garlic cloves, minced

½ cup low-sodium vegetable broth

4 cups finely chopped kale

Mustard Sauce

¼ cup Dijon mustard

2 tablespoons pure maple syrup

1 tablespoon balsamic vinegar

¼ teaspoon black pepper

Yields: 4 to 6 servings
Prep Time: 15 minutes
Cook Time: 20 minutes

1. Put the potatoes in a medium saucepan and add enough cold water to cover. Bring to a boil over medium-high heat and cook until tender, about 10 minutes. Drain the potatoes and shock them in cold water so they don't become mushy. Set aside.

2. Meanwhile, in a large nonstick skillet over medium-high heat, sauté the onion and garlic in the vegetable broth until tender and slightly browned, about 8 minutes. Add the kale and cook until it is wilted, about 5 minutes. Reduce the heat to low and continue cooking for another 5 minutes. Add the potatoes and cook until heated through.

3. In a small bowl, whisk together the mustard sauce ingredients.

4. Drizzle the mustard sauce over the vegetables and serve warm.

Collard Ribbons

This recipe is more about cutting technique than ingredients. Our family never ate many collards until I learned this ribbon style of cutting, which eliminates their tough texture. If you usually just chop them, you'll see that this style of cutting makes a huge difference.

1 bunch collard greens, stems removed

1 red onion, thinly sliced

4 or 5 garlic cloves, minced

1 tablespoon apple cider vinegar

1½ teaspoons pure maple syrup

1 teaspoon smoked paprika

¼ teaspoon sea salt

¼ teaspoon black pepper

Yields: 4 servings
Prep Time: 15 minutes
Cook Time: 5 minutes

1. Stack 4 or 5 collard leaves. Roll the leaves tightly into a long tube. Hold the tube tightly with one hand while you cut very thin crosswise slices with the other. The smaller the cut, the more tender the collards will be—¼-inch-thick ribbons is ideal. Repeat with the remaining collard leaves.

2. In a large nonstick skillet over medium-high heat, sauté the onion and garlic in a small amount of water until the onion begins to soften and caramelize, about 8 minutes. Add the collards, vinegar, maple syrup, paprika, salt, and pepper and sauté for 3 to 5 minutes, just until wilted and bright green. Serve warm.

Chopped Sweet and Sour Brussels Sprouts

Brussels sprouts have a strong flavor that I absolutely love. However, many people (including a few of my family members) struggle with their distinct cabbage flavor. So, I created a recipe that complements them nicely. If you like sweet, sour, and smoky flavors, you will enjoy this dish.

1 pound Brussels sprouts

1 red onion, halved then thinly sliced

4 garlic cloves, minced

¼ cup red wine vinegar

2 tablespoons pure maple syrup

1 teaspoon smoked paprika

¼ teaspoon sea salt

¼ teaspoon black pepper

¼ cup raw pumpkin seeds

Yields: 4 to 6 servings
Prep Time: 15 minutes
Cook Time: 10 minutes

1. Trim the Brussels sprouts and pulse them in a food processor until shredded.

2. In a large nonstick skillet over medium-high heat, sauté the onion and garlic in a small amount of water until the onion starts to turn brown, 8 to 10 minutes. Add the shredded Brussels sprouts, vinegar, maple syrup, paprika, salt, and pepper, reduce the heat to medium, and simmer for 1 to 2 minutes.

3. Top with the pumpkin seeds and serve warm.

Smashed Cauliflower

I'm not a huge fan of plain steamed cauliflower, but mash it up with herbs and spices and I love it. Kids will, too! The herbs and cheesy nutritional yeast really make this dish. It's a fun and healthy substitute for traditional mashed potatoes because it's not only lighter but easier to make.

1 large head cauliflower, chopped into florets

2 tablespoons nutritional yeast flakes

1 tablespoon chopped fresh rosemary

1 teaspoon garlic powder

1 teaspoon dried chives

½ teaspoon sea salt

½ teaspoon black pepper

Yields: 4 servings
Prep Time: 15 minutes
Cook Time: 10 minutes

1. Put the cauliflower in a large pot and add enough water to cover the florets. Bring the water to a boil over medium-high heat, reduce the heat to medium-low, and cook until the cauliflower is tender, 8 to 10 minutes.

2. Drain the cauliflower and return it to the pot. Puree the cauliflower with a potato masher or immersion blender. Gently fold in the nutritional yeast, rosemary, garlic powder, chives, salt, and pepper. Serve warm.

Kim's Hint: *I have made this recipe incorporating a couple of cooked carrots into the mash as well. This adds extra color and flavor to the dish.*

Polenta Fries

We love grits in our family, and leftovers always get turned into these tasty fries. I simply spread out my leftover grits on a baking sheet and refrigerate. Then I slice the chilled grits into matchsticks and roast until crispy and delicious. Serve with ketchup (low sodium/sugar) or your favorite sauce or dressing.

3 cups water

1 cup stone-ground yellow grits

2 teaspoons tahini

1 teaspoon garlic powder

1 teaspoon onion powder

½ teaspoon sea salt

½ teaspoon black pepper

Yields: 4 servings
Prep Time: 15 minutes, plus 1 hour to chill
Cook Time: 40 minutes

1. In a small saucepan, bring the water to a boil over high heat. Add the grits slowly, whisking constantly so they do not become lumpy. Add the tahini, garlic powder, onion powder, salt, and pepper, reduce the heat to medium-low, and stir until thickened, about 10 minutes. Remove from the heat and set aside to cool a bit.

2. Line a baking sheet with parchment paper. Spread the polenta over the prepared baking sheet to a thickness of ½ to 1 inch. Put the baking sheet in the refrigerator and chill for 1 hour.

3. Preheat the oven to 400°F.

4. Remove the baking sheet from the refrigerator and slice the polenta into matchsticks about ½ inch by 3 inches. Spread them out on the parchment so that they are not touching. Bake for 20 to 30 minutes, until they become crispy and slightly golden brown. Serve warm.

Kim's Hints:

- *Polenta fries can be brushed with lime juice and sprinkled with chili powder for extra flavor.*
- *You can also cut the chilled polenta into small cubes, dip them into nutritional yeast flakes, and bake them to make crispy polenta croutons.*

Baked Salt and Vinegar Fries

Traditional French fries are my biggest "high fat" weakness, so I am motivated to cut and bake my own fries that are both healthy and satisfying. This recipe has all the crunchiness of traditional French fries without all the fat.

5 russet potatoes

2 to 3 cups apple cider vinegar

2 tablespoons nutritional yeast flakes

Sea salt

Yields: 4 servings
Prep Time: 10 minutes
Cook Time: 40 minutes

1. Preheat the oven to 425°F. Line a baking sheet with parchment paper.

2. Peel or scrub the potatoes, then cut them lengthwise into ¼-inch-thick slices. Stack a few potato slices at a time and cut them into thin matchsticks.

3. Put the potatoes in a large pot and pour in enough vinegar to cover them. Cook over medium-high heat for 10 minutes. Do not cook the potatoes for any longer than 10 minutes or they will become too soft and will not crisp up in the oven. Drain the potatoes in a colander but do not rinse them.

4. Place the potatoes in a single layer on the prepared baking sheet. Sprinkle them with the nutritional yeast and salt to taste.

5. Bake for 30 minutes, or until golden brown. Serve warm.

Kim's Hint: *I sometimes add fresh or dried dill to the potatoes before baking for a dill pickle flavor.*

Breaded Onion Rings

This recipe was inspired by the canned onion strings on top of a traditional green bean casserole. The canned onions are greasy, salty, and highly processed, and I knew there had to be a delicious alternative. These onion rings are it! In fact, the first time I threw them together, my family ate them all before they even made it to the top of the casserole. I was so excited about the idea of onion rings for casseroles, snacks, and side dishes that I decided to include this recipe in the cookbook.

4 slices 100% whole wheat bread, toasted

1 tablespoon nutritional yeast flakes

2 tablespoons dried parsley

1½ teaspoons garlic powder

1 teaspoon onion powder

1 teaspoon Italian herb blend

½ teaspoon sea salt (optional)

1½ cups whole wheat flour

1 cup unsweetened plant-based milk

2 large red or white onions, cut into ¼-inch-thick slices and separated into rings

Yields: 2 to 3 servings
Prep Time: 20 minutes
Cook Time: 25 minutes

1. Preheat the oven to 425°F. Line a baking sheet with parchment paper.

2. Process the toasted bread slices in a food processor until fine crumbs form. Add the nutritional yeast, parsley, garlic powder, onion powder, Italian herb blend, and sea salt (if using).

3. Transfer the crumb mixture to a shallow dish. Put the flour in another shallow dish, and the milk in a third shallow dish.

4. Completely coat the onion rings with flour, then dip them in the milk, and finally coat them in the bread crumbs. You can do several onions rings at once.

5. Place the breaded onion rings on the prepared baking sheet and bake for 15 to 25 minutes, until golden brown and crispy. Serve warm.

Kim's Hint: *You can save time by starting with 3 cups whole wheat bread crumbs instead of making the crumbs from toast. Or, for gluten-free onion rings, replace the bread crumbs with crushed Rice Chex cereal.*

Holiday Stuffing

When I made stuffing as a kid, it always involved lots of enriched bread, melted butter, vegetables, and sausage. Although it was delicious, I knew I had to create a healthier version for my own family, since this dish was a tradition I wasn't willing to give up.

2 onions, diced

5 celery stalks, diced

8 ounces mushrooms, sliced

4 garlic cloves, minced

1½ cups low-sodium vegetable broth, divided

6 cups cubed 100% whole-grain bread

½ cup chopped pecans

¼ cup finely chopped fresh parsley

1 teaspoon toasted fennel seeds

1 teaspoon dried thyme

1 teaspoon dried sage

½ teaspoon dried marjoram

1 teaspoon sea salt

½ teaspoon black pepper

Yields: 6 to 8 servings
Prep Time: 30 minutes
Cook Time: 30 minutes

1. Preheat the oven to 375°F. Line a 9- by 13-inch baking dish with parchment paper.

2. In a large nonstick skillet over medium-high heat, sauté the onions, celery, mushrooms, and garlic in ½ cup of the vegetable broth until the vegetables are softened, about 8 minutes.

3. Stir in the bread cubes, pecans, parsley, fennel, thyme, sage, marjoram, salt, and pepper and continue cooking for 3 to 5 minutes. Stir in the remaining 1 cup vegetable broth a little at a time until you have the desired moistness. Keep in mind that the stuffing will dry out a bit during the baking process.

4. Spread the stuffing into the prepared baking dish, cover with aluminum foil, and bake for 20 to 30 minutes. Remove the foil and continue baking for another 10 minutes, or until the edges are slightly dry. Serve warm.

Baked Holiday Sweet Potato Casserole

In the traditional holiday casserole, sweet potatoes are smothered in marshmallows and loaded with extra sugars. This is a fruity alternative. It feels more like a dessert than a side dish, but for a Thanksgiving tradition, it's perfect!

3 large sweet potatoes, peeled and cut into cubes (about 5 cups)

2 medium Granny Smith apples, peeled, cored, and diced

1 (8-ounce) can crushed pineapple in juice, undrained

¼ cup canned lite coconut milk

2 tablespoons pure maple syrup

1 teaspoon ground cinnamon

¼ teaspoon ground nutmeg

¼ teaspoon ground ginger

Topping

1 cup oats

½ cup chopped walnuts or pecans

1 cup chopped pitted dates

¼ cup unsweetened applesauce

Yields: 6 to 8 servings
Prep Time: 20 minutes
Cook Time: 50 minutes

1. Preheat the oven to 375°F.

2. In a medium saucepan, combine the sweet potatoes and apples, then pour in enough water to cover them. Bring the water to a boil over medium-high heat, reduce the heat to medium, and cook until the potatoes are tender when pierced with a fork, 10 to 15 minutes. Drain and transfer to a large mixing bowl.

3. Meanwhile, in a small mixing bowl, combine the topping ingredients. The mixture will be somewhat dry. Set aside.

4. Mash the potatoes and apples coarsely with a fork or potato masher. Add the pineapple with its juices, coconut milk, maple syrup, and spices. Mix well.

5. Transfer the potato mixture to an 8-inch square baking dish. Crumble the topping mixture over the sweet potatoes.

6. Bake for 30 to 35 minutes, until the top is golden brown and the potatoes begin to bubble. Serve warm.

> **Kim's Hint:** *The oatmeal-nut topping used here is my go-to topping for fruit crisps such as apple crisp, peach crisp, and strawberry-rhubarb crisp. It's the perfect texture and sweetness every time.*

Cranberry-Date Relish

I usually serve this delicious relish at Thanksgiving and Christmas. The dates give it sweetness without any added sugars.

3 cups fresh cranberries

2 medium apples, peeled, cored, and diced

½ cup chopped pitted dates

½ cup orange juice

¼ cup pure maple syrup

1 tablespoon grated orange zest

1 teaspoon ground cinnamon

½ teaspoon ground ginger

Yields: 2 cups
Prep Time: 10 minutes
Cook Time: 20 minutes

In a medium saucepan, combine all the ingredients and bring to a boil over medium-high heat. Reduce the heat to medium-low and cook until the mixture thickens and the fruits are soft, 15 to 20 minutes. Serve warm or cold.

Desserts

Is One Sugar Best?

Plants contain naturally occurring sugars, which are fine to consume in moderation. Refined sugar, however, is where we can run into trouble. Here I am referring to sugar that has been separated from its whole food source and processed in some way.

Official guidelines suggest that refined sugars should constitute less than 5 percent of our total daily calorie intake. For a normal-weight adult, that's an upper limit of 25 grams a day, or about 6 teaspoons. The average American, however, consumes around 88 grams or 22 teaspoons per day. Just one 12-ounce can of soda contains 40 grams of sugar!

The question everyone asks is: Which sugar is best? We've all heard that refined white sugar is not healthy, but does that mean that pure maple syrup, brown rice syrup, agave nectar, Sucanat, or date sugar are good for you? The bottom line is that you should try to minimize (or even eliminate) your intake of *all* forms of refined sugar. Instead, I recommend using dried and fresh fruits to sweeten your recipes.

What about dessert? I believe desserts should be reserved for birthdays, holidays, and other celebrations, and I've included some favorite recipes here for those special occasions. I definitely don't think anyone should consume dessert daily. If you feel you must have "something sweet" every day, I recommend fresh or frozen fruit. Dried fruits don't contain the fiber and water combination found in fresh fruit, which is important for achieving satiety, so they can too easily be eaten to excess. For this reason, I recommend using dried fruit only as a sweetener in a recipe or as a topping on a dessert or breakfast cereal.

My grandmother always had cookies in her jar or a special dessert waiting after every meal. It was truly her expression of love for her family. Fortunately, there are plenty of other, non-sugary ways to show love . . . like preparing delicious, unprocessed plant-based foods.

Blueberry Cobbler

We live a couple of miles from a big blueberry farm, and the berries I pick tend to overflow to my freezer and make their way into just about every recipe I can sneak them into. I love to use them in a cobbler, and this one is whole-grain, low in sugar, and perfectly gooey!

5 cups blueberries, fresh or frozen

1 tablespoon Sucanat

¼ cup water

2 teaspoons lemon juice

2½ tablespoons cornstarch

1½ cups whole wheat pastry flour

2 teaspoons baking powder

¼ teaspoon sea salt

¼ teaspoon ground nutmeg

¾ cup unsweetened plant-based milk

2 tablespoons pure maple syrup

Yields: 6 servings
Prep Time: 15 minutes
Cook Time: 30 minutes

1. Preheat the oven to 400°F.

2. In a medium saucepan, combine the blueberries, Sucanat, water, lemon juice, and cornstarch. Cook over medium-high heat until bubbly and thickened, about 8 minutes.

3. Spread the blueberry mixture evenly in an 8-inch square baking pan. In a medium mixing bowl, whisk together the flour, baking powder, sea salt, and nutmeg. Add the milk and maple syrup and stir just until moistened.

4. Drop the dough mixture by the tablespoon over the blueberries. You should be able to cover most of the blueberries with the dough.

5. Bake for 25 to 30 minutes, until lightly browned. Serve warm.

Baked Bananas

Bananas are loaded with nutrients and just happen to be naturally sweet and creamy. They also always seem to go from green to ripe overnight. Baked bananas are an easy way to use up those ripened bananas quickly. I often serve these with our favorite plant-based ice cream for a special occasion dessert.

2 tablespoons lime juice

2 tablespoons pure maple syrup

1 tablespoon rum

¼ teaspoon ground cinnamon

⅛ teaspoon ground nutmeg

2 bananas, peeled and sliced lengthwise

Yields: 2 to 4 servings
Prep Time: 10 minutes
Cook Time: 15 minutes

1. Preheat the oven to 400°F. Line a baking sheet with parchment paper.

2. In a small bowl, whisk together the lime juice, maple syrup, rum, cinnamon, and nutmeg.

3. Place the four banana halves on the prepared baking sheet. Brush the syrup sauce evenly over them. Bake for 10 to 15 minutes. Serve warm.

Kim's Hint: *You can replace the rum with ¼ to ½ teaspoon rum flavoring.*

Raspberry Jam Bars

I love date bars and wanted to recreate them using berries. These bars are delicious and easy to make. They're like breakfast in a cookie!

Fruit Filling

- 2 cups frozen raspberries
- 3 tablespoons pure maple syrup
- 1 teaspoon pure vanilla extract
- 3 tablespoons chia seeds

Crumble Mixture

- 2 cups instant oats
- ¾ cup walnuts
- ½ cup Medjool dates, pitted
- ¼ cup Sucanat
- ¼ cup unsweetened applesauce
- ¼ cup water
- ½ teaspoon ground cinnamon
- ½ teaspoon baking soda
- ¼ teaspoon sea salt

Yields: 8 servings
Prep Time: 25 minutes
Cook Time: 30 minutes

1. Preheat the oven to 400°F. Line a 9-inch square baking pan with parchment paper.

2. In a small saucepan, cook the raspberries, maple syrup, and vanilla over medium heat. When the mixture begins to cook down and thicken, stir in the chia seeds. Take the pan off the heat and set aside to thicken.

3. In a food processor, blend the oats, walnuts, and dates until a crumbly and slightly moist mixture forms. Add the applesauce, water, cinnamon, baking soda, and sea salt. Pulse until a thick, crumbly dough forms.

4. Firmly press half of the oatmeal mixture into the prepared pan. Use a spatula to spread the thickened raspberry mixture evenly over the crumble mixture. Top with the remaining oat mixture and press lightly.

5. Bake until golden brown, 25 to 30 minutes. Cool thoroughly and cut into bars.

Grandma's Rhubarb Sauce

My father always grew rhubarb in our garden. Every spring there was so much rhubarb stalk (that's the only part of the plant you can eat) that we made rhubarb pie, cake, sauce, and almost anything we could think of to use it up. This is my mother's recipe for rhubarb sauce. It's a little tart, but I think it's perfect for most cakes and plant-based ice creams. I even like to spread it on toast for breakfast.

¼ cup water

½ cup Sucanat or pure maple syrup

2 cups fresh or frozen (thawed) rhubarb, diced

1 teaspoon grated lemon zest

⅛ teaspoon ground nutmeg

Yields: 2 to 4 servings
Prep Time: 10 minutes
Cook Time: 15 minutes

In a small saucepan, bring the water and Sucanat to a boil over medium heat. Add the rhubarb and cook for 10 to 15 minutes, stirring frequently. When the rhubarb becomes a thick sauce (like applesauce), remove the pan from the heat and stir in the lemon zest and nutmeg. Serve warm or chilled. Store leftovers in an airtight container in the refrigerator for 10 to 14 days.

Kim's Hints:

- *If you're using frozen rhubarb, measure the rhubarb while it is still frozen, then thaw it completely and drain in a colander.*
- *Reducing the sweetener for this recipe is tricky since rhubarb can be very tart. You can always begin with a smaller amount of sweetener and add more as needed.*
- *If you like, you can easily turn this into Strawberry-Rhubarb Sauce by adding a cup of fresh or frozen strawberries to the saucepan.*

Hot Fudge Sundae Cake

This simple yet delicious recipe brings back fond childhood memories. My mom's hot fudge sundae cake was made using white flour and refined sugar, but this healthier version is just as moist, chewy, and rich! When you scoop it out of the pan, you'll be pleasantly surprised at all the fudge underneath. This cake goes nicely with a plant-based ice cream or sliced bananas.

Cake

1 cup whole wheat pastry flour

½ cup Sucanat

2 tablespoons unsweetened cocoa powder

2 teaspoons baking powder

½ teaspoon ground cinnamon

¼ teaspoon sea salt

½ cup unsweetened plant-based milk

¼ cup unsweetened applesauce

1 teaspoon pure vanilla extract

1 cup roughly chopped walnuts

Fudge Topping

½ cup Sucanat

¼ cup unsweetened cocoa powder

1¾ cups hot water

Yields: 6 servings
Prep Time: 15 minutes
Cook Time: 35 minutes

1. Preheat the oven to 350°F.

2. In a large mixing bowl, whisk together the flour, Sucanat, cocoa powder, baking powder, cinnamon, and salt. Add the milk, applesauce, vanilla, and walnuts and stir until combined. Spread the batter into a 9-inch square baking pan.

3. To make the fudge topping, sprinkle the Sucanat and cocoa over the batter in the pan. Pour the hot water over the batter. Bake for 30 to 35 minutes, until the top of the cake is dry. This is a wet, fudgy dessert that needs to be spooned into dessert cups. Serve warm.

Chickpea Chocolate Chip Cookies

These cookies have a wonderful texture and are slightly denser than the chocolate chip cookies in *The PlantPure Nation Cookbook*. They are gluten free and lower in fat since I opted to use powdered peanut butter rather than the traditional creamy peanut butter. You'll need a blender for this recipe, but it's well worth the extra cleanup.

1 tablespoon flax meal or chia seeds

3 tablespoons water

1½ cups oats

½ cup powdered peanut butter

¾ teaspoon baking powder

¾ teaspoon baking soda

¼ teaspoon sea salt

1 cup vegan chocolate chips

1 (15-ounce) can chickpeas, rinsed and drained, or 1½ cups cooked chickpeas

¾ cup unsweetened plant-based milk

2 teaspoons pure vanilla extract

¾ cup Sucanat

Yields: 18 to 24 cookies
Prep Time: 15 minutes
Cook Time: 10 minutes

1. Preheat the oven to 375°F. Line a baking sheet with parchment paper.

2. In a small bowl, mix the flax meal and water and set aside to thicken.

3. In a blender, process the oats into flour. Transfer to a large mixing bowl and add the powdered peanut butter, baking powder, baking soda, salt, and chocolate chips. Mix until thoroughly combined.

4. In the same blender (no need to rinse it out), combine the chickpeas, milk, vanilla, and Sucanat. Blend until very smooth and creamy.

5. Fold the chickpea mixture into the dry ingredient mixture and mix only until combined. Do not overmix.

6. Drop spoonfuls of the cookie dough onto the prepared baking sheet. I like to shape my cookies by dipping a spoon into water, then smoothing out each cookie and pressing slightly. This keeps them uniform and smooth. Bake for 10 to 12 minutes, until dry and lightly golden.

Kim's Hint: *I use PB2 powdered peanut butter. If you can't find it, you can simply use ⅛ cup all-natural peanut butter. This will add to the fat, but you will get a very similar outcome.*

Oatmeal Raisin Mookies

I like to call these "mookies" since they are a cross between a muffin and a cookie. Without the added butters or oils, these cookies don't melt and spread like a typical high-fat cookie. Instead, they have a tender, cakelike texture.

1 tablespoon flax meal or chia seeds

2 tablespoons water

6 tablespoons unsweetened plant-based milk

⅓ cup unsweetened applesauce

¼ cup Sucanat

2 teaspoons pure vanilla extract

1¼ cups oats

1 cup whole wheat pastry flour

¾ teaspoon baking soda

¾ teaspoon baking powder

1 teaspoon ground cinnamon

¼ teaspoon ground nutmeg

⅛ teaspoon ground cloves

½ cup raisins

½ cup vegan chocolate chips

½ cup chopped walnuts

Yields: 18 to 20 cookies
Prep Time: 15 minutes
Cook Time: 10 minutes

1. Preheat the oven to 375°F. Line a baking sheet with parchment paper.

2. In a small bowl, mix the flax meal and water. Set aside to thicken.

3. In a large mixing bowl, combine the milk, applesauce, Sucanat, and vanilla. When the flax meal mixture has thickened, add this to the wet ingredients.

4. In another bowl, whisk together the oats, flour, baking soda, baking powder, cinnamon, nutmeg, and cloves. Mix in the raisins, chocolate chips, and walnuts. Add the dry mixture to the wet ingredients and mix until moistened. Do not overmix, as this will make your cookies tough.

5. Drop spoonfuls of the cookie dough onto the prepared baking sheet. I like to use a wet spoon to flatten and spread the cookies a bit. Bake for 10 to 12 minutes, until dry to the touch and slightly golden.

Mom's Refrigerated Chocolate Pie

This dessert is a family favorite for special occasions. It is every bit as delicious as chocolate cheesecake and is loved by my non-vegan family and friends, too. I almost didn't include this recipe since it is so sweet and rich, but since we do indulge occasionally, I thought you should have the opportunity to try it as well.

1 (14-ounce) package firm tofu

¼ cup unsweetened plant-based milk

⅓ cup pure maple syrup or agave nectar

1 teaspoon pure vanilla extract

½ cup unsweetened cocoa powder

¼ teaspoon sea salt

½ cup vegan chocolate chips, melted

1 recipe No-Bake Pie Crust (page 254)

Yields: 8 servings
Prep Time: 15 minutes, plus 1 hour to chill
Cook Time: 0 minutes

1. Combine the tofu, milk, maple syrup, vanilla, cocoa powder, and sea salt in a blender and blend on high until very smooth. If necessary, you can add a little more milk if you are having trouble blending the mixture. It may take a while, but it should become smooth, creamy, and shiny.

2. Add the melted chocolate chips and blend to incorporate.

3. Pour the mixture into the pie crust and smooth out the surface. (You can also make fancy designs in the surface if you wish.)

4. Put the pie in the refrigerator and chill for 1 to 2 hours, until firm to the touch. Cut and serve to the chocolate fans in your life.

Kim's Hints:
- *You can use a food processor instead of a blender, but you may not get quite as smooth a consistency.*
- *The chocolate chips are what make this pie firm up when refrigerated, so don't even consider leaving them out!*

No-Bake Pie Crust

This pie crust is easy to prepare and can be used for any no-bake pie recipe. I especially like it for my Mom's Refrigerated Chocolate Pie (page 252).

1½ cups oats

1 cup walnuts

1 cup Medjool dates, pitted

¼ cup unsweetened applesauce

½ cup unsweetened coconut flakes

½ teaspoon ground cinnamon

Yields: 1 pie crust
Prep Time: 15 minutes
Cook Time: 0 minutes

1. Grind the oats in a food processor into a grainy flour. Add the walnuts and blend until the mixture is completely combined and sticking together.

2. Add the dates, applesauce, coconut, and cinnamon to form a dough that holds together when you press it. If it feels a bit dry, add a tablespoon at a time of applesauce or water to achieve a stickier consistency.

3. Press the mixture into the bottom and sides of a 9-inch pie pan and fill with a no-bake pie filling.

Pudding Pops

These ice pops are not just for kids—adults love chocolate, too! It's a great way to create a wholesome plant-based frozen treat, especially if you don't have an ice cream maker. I use avocados for the "pudding" effect. The flavor of the avocados is completely overpowered by chocolate, leaving just their creamy texture. Enjoy!

2 avocados, pitted and peeled

½ cup unsweetened cocoa powder

½ cup agave nectar

1 cup unsweetened plant-based milk

2 teaspoons pure vanilla extract

Pinch of sea salt

Yields: 6 ice pops
Prep Time: 25 minutes, plus 4 hours to freeze
Cook Time: 0 minutes

Combine all the ingredients in a blender or food processor and blend until smooth. If you have difficulty getting everything to come together evenly, you can slowly add a little more milk by the tablespoon. Divide the mixture among six ice pop molds and freeze until firm, 4 to 6 hours.

Mango-Coconut Pudding

Serve with fresh seasonal fruit.

2 large mangoes, pitted, peeled, and diced

1 (14-ounce) package firm tofu

½ cup canned lite coconut milk

3 tablespoons pure maple syrup

¼ teaspoon ground cinnamon

⅛ teaspoon ground nutmeg

Yields: 4 to 6 servings
Prep Time: 10 minutes, plus time to chill
Cook Time: 0 minutes

Blend all the ingredients in a food processor or blender until smooth. Transfer to dessert cups and refrigerate until chilled.

Kim's Hint: *You can use 3 cups frozen mango chunks instead of fresh mangoes.*

Frozen Grapes

This hardly counts as a recipe, but these sweet snacks are worth mentioning. Grapes are naturally sweet and freeze beautifully. They have a creamy consistency and are a perfect frozen snack. Some people have compared them to frozen candy. I recommend having them on hand for those sweet cravings.

1 large bunch red grapes, stems removed

Yields: 1 bunch grapes
Prep Time: 5 minutes, plus 1 hour to freeze
Cook Time: 0 minutes

Kim's Hint: *I find that red grapes freeze better than green, but you can certainly use whatever grapes you have on hand.*

Line a rimmed baking sheet with paper towels or wax paper. Wash the grapes and pat dry with a paper towel. Spread them out on the prepared baking sheet, leaving some space between them. Freeze until firm, at least 1 hour, then store in zip-top bags in the freezer.

Berry-Banana Ice Cream

There is no need to go without an occasional frozen treat just because you're eating vegan—frozen bananas make the perfect base for ice cream. Because bananas are naturally sweet, there is no need to add any sugar. If you're trying to impress a dinner guest, make this recipe and top it with coconut flakes and chocolate shavings.

4 frozen bananas

1 cup frozen berries

¼ to ½ cup unsweetened plant-based milk

Yields: 4 servings
Prep Time: 15 minutes
Cook Time: 0 minutes

Combine the frozen bananas, berries, and ¼ cup milk in a blender or food processor. Blend on high until smooth and creamy. Add more milk, a tablespoon at a time, as needed to create a soft and creamy texture. Serve immediately.

Kim's Hints:

- *I like to keep frozen bananas on hand for this ice cream. It's a great way to preserve bananas that are in danger of getting overripe. Simply peel the ripe bananas and slice into chunks. Put the chunks in a zip-top bag and freeze.*
- *Blending this ice cream may take a while if the bananas are frozen solid. You may even want to slightly thaw the bananas first so they are easier to blend.*
- *There is no end to the things you can add to this ice cream. I love to add 2 tablespoons unsweetened cocoa powder and a little maple syrup (if needed) for a delicious chocolate flavor. You can also try frozen mangoes, peaches, or pineapple, since all three go so nicely with bananas.*

Strawberry-Banana Smoothie Pops

Frozen treats can be much healthier than what is sold at the supermarket. I love making these ice pops during the summer months, when berries and fruit are in season and abundant. I have been known to eat these little treasures for breakfast!

1 pound strawberries

1 banana

½ cup unsweetened plant-based milk

½ cup blueberries

Yields: 4 to 6 ice pops
Prep Time: 10 minutes, plus 4 hours to freeze
Cook Time: 0 minutes

Combine the strawberries, banana, and milk in a blender and blend until smooth. If you like a chunkier consistency, stop your blender sooner. I like to see bits of fruit in the ice pops. Slowly pour the smoothie mixture into ice pop molds while adding a few blueberries here and there. Freeze for at least 4 hours, until completely frozen.

Kim's Hints:

- *You might need to run warm water briefly over the molds to get the pops out.*
- *There are many sizes and shapes of ice pop molds available through Amazon or your local store, but you can also use disposable paper cups and Popsicle sticks. You will need to insert the sticks halfway through the freezing process rather than at the beginning, so they don't tip over. Simply peel off the paper cup when you're ready to enjoy your ice pop.*

Acknowledgments

There are many people who helped make this cookbook possible.

A special thanks to my loving husband, Nelson, and our three kids, Whitney, Colin, and Laura. They read, wrote, photographed, and tested the recipes in this book. They are not only my biggest fans, but my strongest foundation in life!

In addition, I would like to thank Jason Boyer, who works on our team at PlantPure. He was our head chef during the local Jumpstarts documented in our film, *PlantPure Nation*, and contributed to many of these recipes, while also giving me inspiration and motivation.

I'd also like to thank Laura Dietrich, our health coach at PlantPure, for sharing and testing recipes as well. Indeed, the efforts of our entire team at PlantPure, along with our many active Pods, are what make it possible for these recipes to reach thousands of people.

My biggest thank you goes to my mother- and father-in-law, Karen and Colin Campbell. Colin's research, passion, and willingness to spread this powerful health message is changing the lives of so many people.

A

Acorn Squash, Stuffed, 205
African Wraps, 79
Almond or Cashew Milk, 34
Apple Butter, Slow Cooker, 143
Artichoke and White Bean Salad, 103
Asian Coleslaw, 104
Asian Noodle Salad, 107
Asian Stewed Tofu, 169
Asparagus Roll-Ups, 131
Avocado-Mango Salad, 108
Aztec Quinoa, 170

B

Baked Bananas, 242
Baked Holiday Sweet Potato Casserole, 237
Baked Salt and Vinegar Fries, 230
Banana(s)
  Baked, 242
  -Berry Ice Cream, 259
  -Strawberry Smoothie Pops, 260
Basil White Bean Sauce, Pasta with, 167
BBQ Sauce, Sweet, 98
Bean(s)
  Black Bean Soup, Easy, 151
  Red Beans and Rice, Creole, 177
  Smoky, 198
  White Bean and Artichoke Salad, 103
  White Bean Basil Sauce, Pasta with, 167
  White Bean Soup, Creamy, 150

Beer Bread, 52
Beet
  Burgers, 64
  Salad, Vibrant Greens and, 123
Bell Peppers, Stuffed, 206
Berry-Banana Ice Cream, 259
Black Bean Soup, Easy, 151
Black Rice Salad with Garden
    Vegetables, 110
Blueberry
  Cobbler, 241
  Corn Cakes, 38
Blue Cheez Dressing, 84
Bourbon Mushrooms, 173
Bread. *See also* Muffins
  Beer, 52
  Cranberry-Orange Nut, 50
  Ginger Yeast, 55
  Pumpkin Raisin Yeast, 53
  Rosemary Garlic, 49
  Spelt, Nutty No-Knead, 46
Breaded Onion Rings, 233
Broccoli
  Salad, Sweet Chile, 121
  Soup, Cream of, 148
Brussels Sprouts, Chopped Sweet and
    Sour, 226
Buffalo-Style Hummus, 128
Burgers
  Beet, 64
  Green Garden, 67
  Sweet Peanut, 68
  Veggie Burger Formula, 63

About the Author

Kim Campbell is the author of *The PlantPure Nation Cookbook* (BenBella Books, 2015), for which she developed over 150 recipes using no processed oils.

Kim works with her husband, Nelson, at PlantPure Wellness, a health and wellness business promoting a whole foods plant-based lifestyle, where she is currently the head of recipe development and culinary education for the Jumpstart program. You can watch her educational videos, in which she covers topics such as label reading, pantry items, restaurant dining, and breakfast ideas, at PlantPureNation.com. She is currently hard at work developing more recipes for the expansion of the PlantPure Nation frozen and dry food line.

Kim graduated from Cornell University with a bachelor's degree in human service studies and a minor in nutrition and child development. She also studied education at the graduate level and went on to a teaching career, working in multiple grades from elementary to high school and teaching a variety of subjects. She is the daughter-in-law of Dr. T. Colin Campbell, considered by many as the "science father" of the rapidly growing plant-based nutrition movement, and shifted to a plant-based lifestyle in her early twenties. She has since raised three children on a plant-based diet. Her passion is creating flavors, textures, and presentations that appeal to mainstream consumers experiencing a plant-based diet for the first time.

THE PLANTPURE NATION COOKBOOK

The Official Companion to the Breakthrough Film

KIM CAMPBELL WITH A FOREWORD BY T. COLIN CAMPBELL, PHD

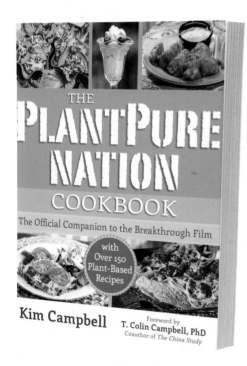

The documentary film *PlantPure Nation* captures the inspiring story of plant-based nutrition's impact on a small town in the rural South and the effort to bring about historic political change. As the film's official companion cookbook, *The PlantPure Nation Cookbook* brings this powerful, science-based approach to nutrition from the big screen to your kitchen with some of the same mouthwatering recipes that kick-started the revolution.

In *The PlantPure Nation Cookbook*, Kim Campbell shares more than 150 extensively tested, 100 percent plant-based recipes that she has created and cultivated over twenty-five years of vegan cooking. She also includes tips, tricks, and grocery lists for people interested in a whole food, plant-based diet. And with intimate background and behind-the-scenes details from the *PlantPure Nation* film, this companion cookbook is a must-have for inspiring healthful eating in your home.

Kim Campbell is the daughter-in-law of Dr. T. Colin Campbell, considered by many as the "science father" of the rapidly growing plant-based nutrition movement. She works with her husband, Nelson, in a health and wellness business promoting a whole-food, plant-based diet. Kim holds a bachelor's degree from Cornell University in Human Service Studies, with a minor in Nutrition and Child Development.

Visit PLANTPURENATION.COM to learn more!

THE CHINA STUDY

The Most Comprehensive Study of Nutrition Ever Conducted

T. COLIN CAMPBELL, PHD, AND THOMAS M. CAMPBELL II, MD

Updated and expanded edition of the bestseller that changed millions of lives

T. Colin Campbell and Thomas M. Campbell II, MD, share the their findings from the most comprehensive study ever undertaken of the relationship between diet and the risk of developing disease: You can dramatically reduce your risk just by changing to a whole foods, plant-based diet.

Featuring brand new content, this heavily expanded edition includes the latest undeniable evidence of the power of a plant-based diet, plus updated information about the changing medical system and how patients stand to benefit from a surging interest in plant-based nutrition.

For more than 40 years, **T. Colin Campbell, PhD**, has been at the forefront of nutrition research. Dr. Campbell is the author of the bestselling book, *The China Study*, the *New York Times* bestseller *Whole*, and *The Low-Carb Fraud* and the Jacob Gould Schurman Professor Emeritus of Nutritional Biochemistry at Cornell University.

Thomas M. Campbell II, MD is a board certified family physician and the co-founder and clinical director of the University of Rochester Program for Nutrition in Medicine. In addition, Dr. Campbell is medical director of the T. Colin Campbell Center for Nutrition Studies, and author of *The China Study Solution*.

Visit THECHINASTUDY.COM to learn more!

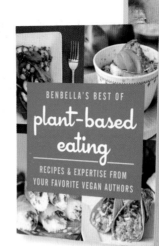